A CHARTWELL-BRATT STU

GW01315926

Pascal Programming and Numerical Methods

For Scientists and Engineers

K R James / W O Riha

School of Computer Studies
University of Leeds

 Chartwell-Bratt

 Studentlitteratur

British Library Cataloguing-in-Publication Data
A catalogue record for this book is available from the British Library.

All rights reserved. No part of this publication may be reproduced or
transmitted in any form or by any means, electronic or mechanical,
including photocopying, recording, or any information storage and retrieval system,
without permission in writing from the publisher.

© K.R. James, W.O. Riha and Chartwell-Bratt 1992.

Chartwell-Bratt (Publishing and Training) Ltd
ISBN 0-86238-303-X

Printed in Sweden
Studentlitteratur, Lund
ISBN 91-44-36061-4

Printing   1 2 3 4 5 6 7 8 9 10 | 1997 96 95 94 93 92

Preface

The Pascal language is widely used as a vehicle for introducing science and engineering students, among others, to structured programming. It is well suited to conveying sound programming technique but avoids burdening the novice with inessential detail or exotic features more relevant to those specializing in computer science. At the same time, many of the available textbooks are designed primarily for computing specialists or, by default, general non-scientific users. It is quite common to find that real numbers make their debut a third of the way through such texts, arrays may appear as a special case of structured data types, and most if not all the examples are studiously non-numerical.

Our aim in this book is to take a different tack. It is possible to teach future scientists and engineers to program competently, even well, without pretending that they will never have to deal seriously with functions of a real variable. The first example of a simple but complete numerical program appears in chapter 1.

The book can realistically be used as the text for a course of 20-25 lectures with supporting practical work. The essentials of Pascal for scientific use are introduced in Part 1 - Elements of Pascal Programming; other interesting aspects of the language are developed in Part 2 - More Advanced Features of Pascal. Once students have covered Part 1 and gained some experience of programming, they should find little difficulty in following the more systematic numerical applications in Part 3 - Approximation and Part 4 - Solution of Equations. From this point of view, the second half of the book provides a wide range of examples to illustrate and reinforce a programming course, and a selection of these topics can be studied in parallel with programming. However, it is also intended to provide a coherent account of the basic numerical methods generally taught to science and engineering students, with the emphasis as much on implementation as on analysis.

As a pedagogic method we favour example over precept. The book contains many annotated program listings, usually with sample output. The programs conform to ISO Pascal level 0 (BS 6192 : 1982). They have been tested on microcomputers and mainframes, and most have been used in introductory courses. Needless to say (but students may need reminding), no one can become competent at programming simply by being told about it; the only way is to do it. Exercises are collected at the end of each part of the book; these are linked to the text, and in the earlier stages involve the modification or development of existing programs.

It is a pleasure to record our thanks to Professor Geoffrey Cook, who read and kindly commented on a first version of the manuscript. We welcome constructive comments from readers and especially those who may find the book of use for teaching.

Ken James   Willi Riha

December 1991

Availability of Software

As an aid to instructors and others, the source codes of some forty example programs used in the book are available on DOS-formatted diskette at a price of £10 inclusive. Please apply to: Dr W.O. Riha, School of Computer Studies, University of Leeds, Leeds LS2 9JT, England.

Contents

Part 4 Solution of Equations

Introduction

These introductory remarks are intended as an orientation for the newcomer to computing. Anyone who has had some previous experience of programming can safely skim the next few pages.

What is a Computer?

The term *computer* refers to a device (for practical reasons, electronic) employed to perform tasks under the control of stored sets of instructions known as *programs*. A washing machine can be 'programmed', but we would not normally think of it as a computer because the repertoire of 'laundry programs' is relatively simple and cannot be modified or extended by the user. Special purpose machines for playing chess or bridge might be called computers, but these are in a similar class; they house just one (very complex) program, the result of years of development effort. In such cases the programs have been written by the designers and built into the machines. Rather than these, we shall be concerned with *general purpose computers* which, depending on the programs we provide and the data we supply, may be used to solve mathematical problems, play a respectable game of chess, attempt with perhaps less success to forecast the weather, monitor the vital signs of intensive care patients, and carry out many other tasks.

Until the seventies most computers were large *mainframes*, often serving hundreds of users 'off-line' (and if the users received their output back the same day they were lucky). Today we have much smaller but no less powerful *minicomputers* with workstations, and self-contained *microcomputers*. You may be using a terminal linked to a mainframe, or you may have a workstation or a micro at your disposal, but whatever the arrangements the same basic principles apply.

The physical components of a computer are called the *hardware*, as opposed to the programs that make it work which are known as *software*. To use a computer you do not need to know about electronics or understand the detailed functioning of the hardware, but it is helpful to be aware of a few basic facts.

1

Every general purpose computer has at least:

(1) a central *processor*, the brain which performs the actual computation and controls all the other components;

(2) a short-term memory, variously known as RAM (*random access memory*) or *core store* - the part of the computer's memory that holds programs and data temporarily while you are working with them;

(3) secondary storage, usually on magnetic *disk*, to save programs, data and other information for future use as long as required;

(4) input and output devices, most likely *keyboard*, *monitor* and probably printer, to communicate with the outside world.

What is Programming?

A computer by itself is an *idiot savant*. All it can do is some basic logical and arithmetical operations such as adding and multiplying numbers, but it can do these extremely fast and never gets them wrong (hardware failures, although possible, are so rare that they can be discounted for most practical purposes). To make the computer do what we want, we have to provide it with a set of precise, detailed and unambiguous instructions - a *program* - which tells the machine exactly how to do the job using the basic operations as building blocks. Programming consists of developing such instructions with the aim of covering every forseeable contingency for the application in question (this is where the notorious 'computer errors' come in).

In the earliest days of computing, programmers had to instruct a computer in its native language, the so-called *machine language*. Even today the only kind of instructions or data that the processor can actually handle are patterns of electronic states which may be visualized as sequences of 0's and 1's called *bits* (binary dig*its*). Such patterns come in units of fixed length (usually 8) called *bytes*, and groups of bytes (2 or 4 depending on the processor) known as *words*. For example, the pattern 0110000000101010 is a 16-bit word which might represent part of a number, a couple of characters (a* in this case) or some coded command that the processor can obey.

Originally, programming in machine language involved preparing and entering a list of such patterns. This could be an interesting exercise, but it was naturally very time-consuming and error-prone. It was for this reason that *assembly languages* were invented; these made it possible for programmers to express the same instructions in some symbolic form instead of as bit patterns. For each make of computer, a special program called an *assembler* would be written to perform the necessary translation into machine code. However, assembly languages soon proved to be too cumbersome for larger problems, and so *high-level languages* began to be developed in the mid-fifties (one of the earliest of these, FORTRAN, is still in use today, albeit heavily revised and extended).

In a high-level language, instructions are expressed in a form intended for the convenience of people and the problems they wish to address rather than computers. For example, x := a+b might be an instruction to calculate the sum of two symbolically-designated numbers and save the result (in general this would translate into several commands at machine level). Such high-level instructions mean nothing to the processor and so cannot be obeyed directly. In order for a high-level instruction to be recognized and obeyed, it has first to be translated into machine code. This is accomplished by special programs known as *compilers* or *interpreters*, which check the *source program* and, provided no language errors are found, carry out the translation (compilers deal with the source program as a whole whereas interpreters translate and execute one instruction at a time).

To date, several hundred high-level programming languages have been developed. The language we are going to describe - one of the most widely used for teaching programming - is Pascal, specifically designed by its author Niklaus Wirth to instil sound principles of programming. (For the record: *Blaise Pascal*, 1623-62, eminent mathematician, scientist, theologian etc, invented what was probably the first calculating machine in 1641.) A number of versions of the Pascal language are in use, differing in some extra facilities they offer; we shall adhere to the ISO standard which should be acceptable to all compilers.

What Do You Do?

When you first switch on your computer or terminal and are ready to start work, you will be communicating with the computer's *operating system*. If you are in a multi-user environment you will have to introduce yourself to the system first by *logging in*; the procedure necessary to get started will be explained by your instructor. The operating system is a supervisory program which is active all the time, performing basic but important functions such as recognizing when keys have been pressed, making sure that the monitor screen is regularly updated, and generally waiting for commands that it can understand and obey. In this mode a system *prompt* will be displayed on the screen, indicating that the operating system is ready to accept your commands.

One of the first things you will have to learn is how to create and edit *files*. Programs, often data and results, and text in general are held in files, usually on disk; for example, this book was prepared on a microcomputer and the text and figures stored in disk files. An *editor* is a systems program which enables you to create a named file to hold anything that you care to type in. You may enter a Pascal program and, having completed it, exit from the editor. (Modern facilities often provide an 'integrated programming environment' which, once initiated from the system prompt, allows you to edit, compile and execute programs by menu selection entirely within this environment.)

Now that you have a file containing what you believe to be a Pascal program, you can issue a command for the program to be *compiled*. What is quite likely to happen at this stage is that a list of *compilation error messages* appears on the screen. This means that your program was not correct Pascal after all; you missed out a semicolon or typed begun instead of begin (it is worth noting that one or two genuine errors near the top of a program can set off an avalanche of spurious error messages below). You return to the program file, make the necessary changes using the editor commands, exit the editor and try again. All being well, compilation will be successful and the program can be *executed*. There may now be *runtime errors* such as attempted division by zero - you overlooked this possibility when you wrote the program - and execution stops with an error message. You will have to go back to the program file and correct it using the editor. There are software aids available for this 'debugging' process which can help you pinpoint where execution went wrong.

Sooner or later you will have ironed out the obvious bugs; the program runs without a hitch, output appears on the screen or is sent to a file, and execution terminates. This is an encouraging development, but it is no guarantee that the results make sense. The computer does not know what you 'really' want; it can only do as you tell it and that is exactly what it does, faithfully following the instructions specified in your program using the data you supply. The results are no more than you could have produced yourself if you had followed the same instructions literally step by step without making a single mistake. The effects, however, may be different - sometimes surprisingly different - from what you intended. To envisage the effects without actually doing the job yourself is of the essence of good programming. It requires a logical approach, a certain imagination and plenty of practice. Quite apart from the importance of the applications, this can be an enjoyable and rewarding activity in itself, at least when you get it right. But that is another story - the subject of this book.

> But the principal failing occurred in the sailing
> And the Bellman, perplexed and distressed,
> Said he *had* hoped, at least, when the wind blew due East
> That the ship would *not* travel due West!
>
> LEWIS CARROLL, *The Hunting of the Snark*

Part 1

Elements of Pascal Programming

1. Programs

1.1 Program Structure

All Pascal programs, however long they may be, conform to the same structural design. It is useful to bear this in mind and learn to see the high-level structure - the skeleton of a program - when you are confronted with apparently complicated examples or when you start writing your own. The structure is:

> program *name* (list of *program parameters*);
>
> label
>   List of any statement labels;
>
> const
>   Definition of any *constants* used in the program;
>
> type
>   Definition of any non-standard *data types*;
>
> var
>   Declaration of *variables* with *type specifications*;
>
> Declaration of any *subprograms*, i.e. *functions* or *procedures*;
>
> begin
> *statements*
> end.

The terms in *italics* will be explained in the first six chapters of this book.

The order above is fixed, although some parts may be omitted. For example, we shall have very little use for statement labels, so our programs will contain no label section. There may often be no program constants. In example 1.1 below there are no type or var sections and no subprograms are declared (admittedly this makes it of little practical use). It is even possible for a program to contain no statements. But in all cases there must be a heading specifying at least a name for the program, and a begin end. Thus the simplest Pascal program would be as follows (the final full stop is part of every program and is compulsory).

```
program DoNothing;
begin
end.
```

This can be compiled, i.e. it is a valid program. It is aptly named: it does nothing when executed.

   You will notice that certain words - program, const, type, var, begin, end - appear in bold type. These are called *reserved words* and they play a special role in Pascal. When you create a file containing a program, you will enter such words in ordinary type using either capital or lower-case (small) letters. Many programmers when on their best behaviour employ capital letters for reserved words because this highlights the structure and is an aid to readability. This practice is purely a matter of style. Standard Pascal makes no distinction between capital and lower-case letters in a program; so, for example, BEGIN is the same as begin.

   Here is a program that actually does something (although not a lot). Read it, but do not bother too much about the details yet.

Example 1.1

```
program Sum (output);
(* This program outputs the value of a positive integer n,
   followed by the sum of the first n even integers,
   2 + 4 + ... + 2n = n(n+1)  *)

const
   n = 10;              (* a positive integer that can be altered
                           by editing the program file *)
begin
write(n);              (* outputs the value of n *)
write(' ');            (* outputs a space *)
write(n*(n+1))         (* outputs the value of n(n+1) -
                          the symbol * denotes multiplication *)
end.
```

Notes:
(1) There is one program parameter, output, which normally has the effect of directing the computer output to the monitor screen.
(2) The layout - indentation, insertion of blank lines etc - can be varied at will. The aim is always to present a program so it is easily readable with the structure displayed as clearly as possible.

(3) A *comment* is one or more lines of explanatory text enclosed in comment brackets { }, or the alternative (* *) which will be used throughout this book for reasons of readability. Comments make no difference to the execution of a program (the compiler ignores them), but they are more than a pedantic gloss; well-chosen comments are essential to our understanding of a program.

(4) Between `begin` and `end` there is a sequence of *statements* separated by semicolons (no semicolon appears before an `end`). Statements can run on to more than one line, or there may be several on the same line. In this program, which is a very simple example, there are just three `write` statements which send successively an integer value, a space and another integer value to `output` (the details of this will be explained later).

Test run:
```
10 110
```

[This is the unremarkable output which, together with some system messages, appears on the screen when the program is executed. The exact spacing may be different on your system.]

1.2 Variables and Expressions

In order to refer to objects such as constants in a program, or indeed the program itself, we require a name or *identifier*. An identifier is a letter (capital or lower-case), optionally followed by any sequence of letters and/or digits (the only restriction is that reserved words such as `begin`, `end` etc may not be used as identifiers). Examples of valid identifiers are: `DoNothing`, `Sum`, `n`, `x1`, `x2`. These are all distinct; on the other hand, `al` and `Al` would be the same (why?). It is strongly recommended, although not required, that reasonably succinct names be chosen to reflect the meanings of the objects in question.

One of the most important uses of identifiers is to give names to program *variables*. This is illustrated in the next example.

Example 1.2
The value of the integral $I = \int_0^1 \sin(x^2)\, dx$ is a definite real number, but it cannot be found by any transformation or substitution. However, we know that the value is equal to the area under the curve $y = \sin(x^2)$ from $x=0$ to $x=1$; we can estimate it by computing an approximation to this area. A simple way of doing this is by the basic *rectangle* or *mid-point rule*:
(1) find the mid point of the range of integration, $m = (0+1)/2$;
(2) compute the area $(1-0)\times\sin(m^2)$ and take this as an approximation to I.

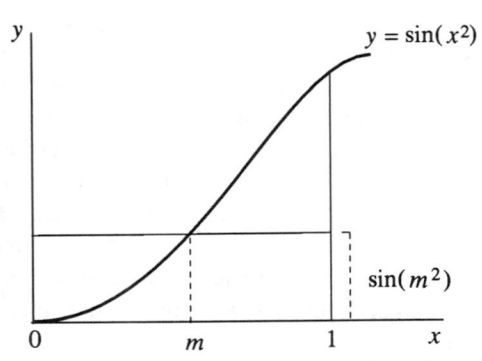

Figure 1.1 The basic rectangle rule

We shall implement this in a slightly more general form as a Pascal program.

```pascal
program Rectangle (output);
(* This program computes an approximation to the integral of
   sin(x^2) from x=a to x=b using the basic rectangle rule *)
const           (* On computers there is an important distinction
                   between REAL NUMBERS (with decimal point) and
                   INTEGERS (whole numbers). The limits of integration
                   a and b are defined here as real constants *)
   a = 0.0;  b = 1.0;
var             (* The two variables used in the program are declared
                   and their types are specified - both are real *)
   midpoint, area : real;
begin           (* Start of actual computation *)
midpoint := (a+b)/2;
area := (b-a)*sin(sqr(midpoint));
write(area)
end.
```

Notes:

(1) The advantage of the **const** definition is that the values of a and b can be altered if required by editing the program file; as the constants are defined in one place near the top of the program, this is easy to do.

(2) The symbol := (obtained on the keyboard by keying : followed by =) is the *assignment symbol*; its effect will be explained below.

(3) sin and sqr are *functions* provided in Pascal; more will be said about these in a later chapter.

Test run:

```
2.4740e-01
```

[The result appears in *e notation*: 2.4740e-01 stands for 2.4740 multiplied by 10 to the power −1; that is, 0.24740. This is only a rough approximation to the integral; later we shall see how to improve it.]

Expressions

Constructs such as

```
n*(n+1)
(a+b)/2
```

are called *arithmetic expressions*. They correspond in a fairly natural way to mathematical formulae. To build up arithmetic expressions we can use the *arithmetic operators*

```
+    -
*    /
```

together with matching pairs of parentheses ( ). The main points to note are:

(1) The operator * must appear explicitly wherever multiplication is required. The usual mathematical abbreviations n(n+1) or even 2n are not valid in Pascal and will not be accepted by the compiler.

(2) Operators of equal priority such as * and / are evaluated from *left to right* in an expression. Thus 4/2*2 would be evaluated as (4/2)*2 = 4, which is almost certainly not what you want. The left-to-right rule can be overridden by parentheses; use a/(b*c) if this is intended.

Unlike a constant definition, which introduces a value along with a name, a variable declaration introduces a name but no value. A variable only has a value if it is given one, either by means of an input statement (see chapter 2) or by explicit assignment. Such a case is

```
midpoint := (a+b)/2
```

known as an *assignment statement*. When executed, this causes the expression on the right to be evaluated and its value to be assigned to the variable on the left. This is only meaningful if the objects appearing on the right have a value; in example 1.2 this is certainly true.

A (simple) variable is often visualized as a *slot* (actually a location in the computer memory) which may currently contain a value or may be empty. An assignment statement can then be thought of as placing a value into a specified slot; when this happens, any previous value that may have been in the slot is lost. This model is helpful in making sense of assignments such as

$$area := area + 0.5$$

What happens here is that the current value of the variable area is looked up; this number is increased by 0.5, and the result is then deposited back into the slot for area. The net effect, therefore, is to increment the value of the variable area by 0.5. Incrementation processes of this sort may be performed many times over, with cumulative effect, during the execution of a program. If an attempt is made to retrieve the value of an *uninitialized* variable - one that has not been given a value - then many modern systems will stop execution with the runtime error *undefined variable*. Beware if your Pascal system does not detect this; make sure that any variables your program needs to look up are properly initialized before you use them. (On the other hand, there is no need to initialize everything in sight.)

Look again at the example programs and see how the syntactic elements are employed. The programs are very simple: they compute a value, output the result and stop. It is scarcely worth using the power of the computer to do this. The main reason why the programs are so trivial is that they lack the feature of *iteration* or controlled repetition. Control structures to perform iteration will be taken up in chapters 2 and 3.

2. Data Types

2.1 Type Integer

Constants or variables which are intended to stand for whole numbers (without decimal point) will normally be of type *integer* in Pascal. We have already seen in example 1.1 how to *define* (that is, specify the name and set a value for) an integer constant. A slightly more complicated case would be

```
const
    m = -1;
    n = 10;
    minusn = -n;
```

A constant can be used in further definitions as soon as it has been defined, as is done in the last line. However, in standard Pascal more general arithmetic expressions are not permitted at this stage.

Integer variables, like all other variables in a program, must be *declared* in the var section. A possible declaration of integer variables might be

```
var
    i, k1, k2, NumberOfItems : integer;
```

Commas are used to separate the names of the variables, and a semicolon terminates the declaration; this may be followed by other declarations in the same var section.

Integer values are stored in exact form in the computer, and the arithmetic operators + - * give exact results when applied to integer operands. However, there is a limit to the size of integer that the computer can handle. The allowed range is

```
-maxint, ..., -1, 0, 1, ..., maxint
```

where maxint is a *predefined constant* (that is, a constant available to all Pascal programs without needing to be defined). The value of maxint depends on the computer and the Pascal implementation. You can find what it is on your system by executing the following simple program.

```
program MaxInteger (output);
begin
write(maxint)
end.
```

The value is quite large, typically around 10^9. On most systems, an attempt to compute or store an integer value outside this range results in the runtime failure *integer overflow* and execution stops.

There is a division operator `div` (obtained by keying the three characters `div` on the keyboard) which applies only to integer operands. It yields an integer result with any remainder discarded. For example,

$$7 \ \mathbf{div} \ 2 = 3 \qquad 5 \ \mathbf{div} \ 3 = 1$$

The related operator `mod` gives the remainder after integer division:

$$7 \ \mathbf{mod} \ 2 = 1 \qquad 5 \ \mathbf{mod} \ 3 = 2$$

(the second operand of a `mod` operation must be positive; if b is not positive, then a `mod` b will result in a compilation or runtime error).

Finally there is the 'real division' operator / which gives a non-integer result, often inexact because of rounding:

$$7/2 = 3.5 \qquad 5/3 = 1.6666...$$

2.2 The For Statement

This is the simplest way of implementing an *iteration loop* in a program. The `for` statement causes a subordinate statement or group of statements to be executed repeatedly a specified number of times. The general form is

```
for i := m to n do
    begin
    statements
    end
```

where i stands for an integer variable called the *control variable*, and m and n stand for constants, variables or expressions of type `integer` (the type can be generalized slightly but no harm will be done if you think in terms of `integer`).

The main points to note about `for` statements are:

(1) The `begin` and `end` bracket several statements into a *compound statement* governed by the controlling `for` (`begin` and `end` can be omitted if only one statement is involved). Indentation should be used to make the control structure clear.

(2) The statement(s) are executed repeatedly with the control variable taking on consecutive values m, m+1, ..., n. If m > n the loop is not entered at all and

execution passes on to the next statement.

(3)   For obvious reasons, statements inside a **for** loop are not allowed to alter the value of the control variable, but they can make use of its current value.

(4)   When the **for** statement is 'exhausted' and execution passes on, the value of the control variable becomes *undefined*. Attempting to make use of its value then will result in the runtime failure *undefined variable* (some non-standard compilers may allow this, but it is an unsafe practice and should be avoided).

A **for** statement is often preceded by the initialization of some variable or variables which are then incremented within the iteration loop. For example, the following program fragment will compute the sum of the first n integers and the sum of the first n squares (where n is a constant or variable with a positive integer value).

```
suml := 0;   sum2 := 0;
for k := 1 to n do
    begin
    suml := suml + k;
    sum2 := sum2 + sqr(k)
    end
```

Compare this with the general form given above and make sure you understand how it works. What would be the effect if n had the value 0 ?

There is a variant **for** statement which is occasionally useful for iterating backwards,

```
for i := m downto n do
. . . . . . . . . . . .
```

Here i takes on the values m, m-1, ..., n (if m < n the loop is bypassed).

2.3 Type Real

The integers by themselves are not sufficient for most mathematical and scientific computations. Also required are numbers with decimal point, to represent (at least approximately) continuously variable quantities such as length and time. Such numbers are stored differently from integers in the computer; they are said to be of type *real*.

We have seen in example 1.2 how to define constants and declare variables of type real:

```
const
    a = 0.0;   b = 1.0;
var
    midpoint, area : real;
```

A real constant is written with a decimal point and at least one digit (possibly a zero) before and after it. We may also employ the *e notation*,

```
const
    h = 0.66253e-33;    (* Planck's constant *)
```

The symbol e-33 denotes 'times 10 to the power −33', and its use is clearly preferable to writing thirty-three zeros.

The arithmetic operators

```
+  -  *  /
```

can be used in an obvious way with parentheses to form real expressions. Because there is a real number equivalent to every integer, it is permissible to write assignment statements such as

```
midpoint := 1;
area := 2*area
```

(the expression on the right is evaluated as a real number and the result is assigned to the real variable on the left). On the other hand, for integer variables i and j, the attempted assignments

```
i := 4.56;
j := area
```

cannot be interpreted unambiguously and will give rise to a compilation error. To make assignments of this sort, the right hand side must be converted to an integer value by means of the Pascal functions round or trunc (see section 5.1).

The set of real numbers representable on the computer, like the set of integers, is limited in range. Although the range is much greater than for integers, *overflow* is still possible. There is no constant maxreal in standard Pascal, but you can find an approximate value on your system by running program MaxReal given at the end of this section. This is one program guaranteed to fail when executed! Before it does so, it outputs a long list of numbers in e notation, and the last number written before overflow failure is the maximum real number to within a factor of 2. Study the program to see how it works.

Since no computer has infinite storage capacity, only numbers of finite length can be represented. In practice this means that real numbers on the computer are restricted to a fixed, maximum number of significant figures known as the *precision* (the equivalent of 8 - 17 decimal digits on most computers). Real numbers with too many figures are rounded to fit. Many mathematical real numbers such as π, 1/3 and even 1/10 cannot be represented exactly on the computer, and indeed most calculations with real numbers are subject to unavoidable *rounding error*. This has important consequences for numerical computation. A more detailed account, which you could profitably look at now, is given in the first part of section 14.2.

```
program MaxReal (output);
var
    x : real;
    i : integer;
begin
x := 1;
for i := 1 to 10000 do
    begin
    writeln(x);
    x := 2*x
    end
end.
```

2.4 Iteration in Action

We return to the numerical integration problem of example 1.2 and ask how the approximation to $\int_0^1 \sin(x^2)\,dx$ can be improved. One way is to divide the range of integration into n equal subintervals (where n may be any positive integer, the larger the better), fit a rectangle in each subinterval by the mid-point method, and add up the areas of all n rectangles. This would be extremely tedious to carry through by hand but is simple with an iterative program.

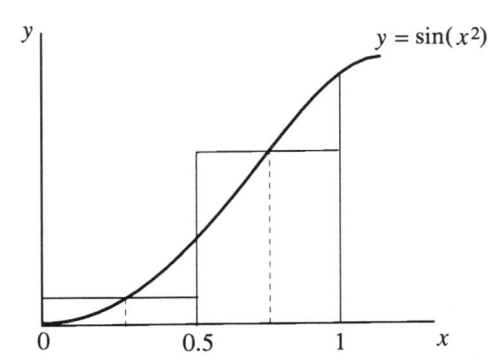

Figure 2.1 The composite rectangle rule with $n=2$

Example 2.1

```
program Integral (input, output);
(* This program computes an approximation to the integral of
   sin(x^2) from x=a to x=b using the rectangle rule with n
   subintervals. The limits of integration a and b are program
   constants, n is read in as data *)
```

```
const
   a = 0.0;  b = 1.0;

var
   i, n         : integer;
   area, h, x   : real;

begin
read(n);           (* input the number of subintervals - a positive
                        integer value must be entered at runtime *)
h := (b-a)/n;     (* calculate width of each subinterval *)
area := 0;        (* initialize area variable to 0 *)
(* Now accumulate total area of n rectangles *)
for i := 1 to n do
   begin
   x := a + (i-0.5)*h;              (* mid point of i-th subinterval *)
   area := area + h*sin(sqr(x))     (* add in area of i-th rectangle *)
   end;
writeln('The rectangle rule with n = ', n);
writeln('Estimate of integral is  ', area)
end.
```

Notes:

(1)   For the first time we have used an input statement, read(n), and a program parameter input to go with it. The parameters input and output appear at the top of most programs.

(2)   Two standard data types integer and real are used. The variables i and n, which are intended to represent whole numbers, are declared as type integer. All variables in the program must be declared in the **var** section.

(3)   The computation is implemented as a short sequence of statements which perform the following tasks:

> read in the value of n;
> calculate the stepwidth h;
> add up the area of n rectangles;
> output the result, then stop.

(4)   The statement

```
writeln('Estimate of integral is  ', area)
```

causes a string of *text* to be output, followed on the same line by the *value* of area, followed by a new line. In earlier programs we have used write, which does the same except that the output position does not move to a new line at the end. Further information on the use of output statements is given in section 3.3.

Test run:

<u>10</u>
```
The rectangle rule with n = 10
Estimate of integral is   3.0982e-01
```

[The first number 10 is the data entered by the user when the program is executed. Here and elsewhere we employ <u>underlining</u> to indicate user input. The second and third lines are the output produced by the program.]

Example 2.2
This is a development of the program in example 2.1. It employs a more flexible method of specifying the integrand, is more 'user friendly' and offers repeated calculations of the integral in one execution of the program.

```
program ImprovedIntegral (input, output);
(* This program computes approximations to the integral of f(x)
   from a to b using the rectangle rule with n subintervals.
   The integrand is specified in function f below; a and b are
   constants, n is read in as data *)
const
   a = 0.0;  b = 1.0;

var
   i, n    : integer;
   area, h : real;

function f (x : real) : real;
(* This is a 'subprogram' defining the integrand *)
   begin
   f := sin(sqr(x))
   end;

begin      (* main program *)
writeln;
writeln('Numerical integration by rectangle rule ...');
writeln;
write('Enter number of subintervals:  '); read(n);
while n > 0 do
   begin
   h := (b-a)/n;
   area := 0;
   for i := 1 to n do
      area := area + h*f(a+(i-0.5)*h);
```

```
      writeln('Computed approximation = ', area);
      writeln;
      write('Another go? Enter number of subintervals (0 to quit): ');
      read(n)
      end
end.
```

Notes:

(1) The integrand $f(x)$ is specified as a function subprogram f (see chapter 5). The main program can then refer to the function f instead of using an explicit formula, which makes it more general.

(2) The operation of the **while** statement here is fairly obvious; the details will be explained in the next chapter.

Test run:

```
Numerical integration by rectangle rule ...

Enter number of subintervals:  100
Computed approximation =  3.1026e-01

Another go? Enter number of subintervals (0 to quit): 500
Computed approximation =  3.1027e-01

Another go? Enter number of subintervals (0 to quit): 1000
Computed approximation =  3.1027e-01

Another go? Enter number of subintervals (0 to quit): 0
```

[The approximations appear to be converging as n increases, a necessary requirement if the numerical method is to be useful.]

3. Control Structures

The power of a programming language is enormously enhanced by provisions for altering the sequential flow of control. If it were not possible to execute statements conditionally - that is, depending on the truth or falsity of some relation - or if the only means of implementing loops were the **for** statement, then a great many computational problems could not be tackled at all. First we require a data type to represent truth values.

3.1 Type Boolean

To represent the outcome of tests in a program we use the *boolean* (truth) *values* `true` and `false` (these are constants of the standard data type `boolean`, just as 0 and 1 are constants of type `integer`). We may declare *variables* and construct *expressions* of type `boolean`, which can then take on only the two truth values. For example, if n is an integer variable with the value 1, then the relation (*boolean expression*) $n > 0$ has the value `true`.

In forming boolean expressions the following *relational operators* may be used:

$$> \qquad >= \qquad =$$
$$< \qquad <= \qquad <> \quad \text{(not equal to)}$$

Some of these consist of two symbols; two keys on the keyboard are required. In addition we may use the *boolean operators*

and   or   not

to form composite expressions. The boolean operators have a higher priority than the relational operators, but this can be overridden by parentheses as in the expression

$$(n >= 1) \textbf{ or } (n <> 0)$$

The operator **or** corresponds to the connector $\lor$ in logic and means *either* or *both*; thus, when $n=1$, the expression $(n >= 1)$ **or** $(n <> 0)$ has the value `true` (in fact this expression is `false` for only one value of n - what is it?)

21

A boolean expression may be used on the right hand side of a *boolean assignment statement*; for example,

```
finished := (n=20) or converged
```

Here, n would be an integer variable, while finished and converged would be boolean variables. Such assignments frequently appear in iteration loops controlled by while or repeat statements (to be discussed in section 3.2).

Example 3.1

The value of a boolean expression is either true or false. Given the truth values of the individual components, we can work out the truth value of the expression itself; the results are often presented as a so-called truth table. The following program outputs the truth table for a boolean expression of three boolean variables.

```
program TruthTable (output);
(* This program outputs the truth table for a boolean expression
   defined in function b below *)

var
   p, q, r : boolean;

function b (p, q, r : boolean) : boolean;
(* This is a subprogram defining a boolean expression *)
   begin
   b := (p or q) and (not (r or q))
   end;

begin      (* main program *)
writeln('Truth table for');
writeln('b = (p or q) and (not (r or q))');
writeln;  writeln;
writeln('   p      q      r         b');
writeln;
for p := false to true do
   for q := false to true do
      for r := false to true do
         writeln(p:7, q:7, r:7, b(p,q,r):10)
end.
```

Notes:

(1) Type boolean is one of the allowed types for the control variable of a for statement referred to in section 2.2.

(2) The for statement is *nested* to a depth of 3; as each inner loop is exhausted, the control variable of the next outer loop is incremented.

(3) Truth values cannot be input by a read statement - there is no genuine need for this - but they can be output by a write statement. The significance of the specifications :7 and :10 will be explained in section 3.3.

Test run:

```
Truth table for
b = (p or q) and (not (r or q))

    p      q      r         b
  false  false  false     false
  false  false  true      false
  false  true   false     false
  false  true   true      false
   true  false  false      true
   true  false  true      false
   true  true   false     false
   true  true   true      false
```

[It can be seen that this particular boolean expression has the value true in only one case out of the possible eight.]

3.2 If, While and Repeat Until

Pascal provides the if statement to express a conditional or branching structure. An if statement takes the general form

```
if boolean expression then
    statement1
else
    statement2
```

Either or both of the two statements may be compound; for example,

```
if y > z then
    begin
    max := y;  min := z
    end
else
    begin
    max := z;  min := y
    end
```

The effect of this is that the statements in the 'then' branch will be executed if y > z, otherwise the statements in the 'else' branch will be executed. In either case execution then passes on to the statement, if any, immediately following the entire if statement. The 'else' branch can be omitted if it is not required. Thus the fragment above could be written equivalently as

```
max := z;   min := y;
if y > z then
   begin
   max := y;   min := z
   end
```

Iteration loops more general than those that can be implemented using for statements are provided by while and repeat statements. A while statement takes the general form

```
while boolean expression do
   statement
```

where *statement* is usually compound. If *boolean expression* is intially false, the loop is bypassed. Otherwise the statement (simple or compound) is executed repeatedly as long as *boolean expression* remains true. In order for the loop to terminate, it is clearly necessary that *boolean expression* should eventually become false; thus there must be at least one statement in the body of the loop which alters the truth value of *boolean expression* (see example 2.2). On exit, execution passes on to the next statement after the while loop.

Sometimes it is more convenient to place the controlling test at the end of the loop. This is the purpose of the repeat statement:

```
repeat
   statements
until boolean expression
```

(a begin and end would be redundant here). The repeat statement performs a similar task to the while statement except that the body is always executed at least once, and this is repeated until *boolean expression* is found to be true.

A for statement is normally used when the number of times a loop is to be executed is known in advance; repeat and while, on the other hand, are more general (and also more powerful) in that the number of iterations need not be known beforehand. We illustrate the use of if, repeat and for statements to perform quite a lengthy computation although the program itself may be short. In later chapters many more illustrations will be found.

Example 3.2
The Collatz sequence $\{x_k\}$ for a positive integer n is constructed by the rule

$$x_0 = n,$$

$$x_{k+1} = \begin{cases} x_k/2 & \text{if } x_k \text{ is even} \\ 3x_k + 1 & \text{if } x_k \text{ is odd} \end{cases}$$

terminating as soon as $x_k = 1$. Thus, starting with $x_0 = 3$, we obtain the sequence 10, 5, 16, 8, 4, 2, 1. The number of terms is called the *height* of x_0; in our example this is 7. Nobody has succeeded in proving that every Collatz sequence is finite, but for the purposes of the following program we assume this to be the case.

```
program Collatz (output);
(* This program finds an integer m in the range 3<=m<=nmax
   which has maximum height, i.e. a longest Collatz sequence *)
const
   nmax = 10000;
var
   n, x, m, height, maxheight : integer;
begin
writeln('Integer <= ', nmax, ' with longest Collatz sequence ...');
writeln;  writeln('    Integer   Height');  writeln;
maxheight := 0;
for n := 3 to nmax do
   begin
   height := 0;  x := n;
   repeat     (* construct the sequence for n *)
      if odd(x) then
         x := 3*x+1
      else
         x := x div 2;
      height := height + 1
   until x = 1;       (* being optimistic! *)
   if height > maxheight then
      begin
      maxheight := height;  m := n;
      writeln(n:9, height:9)
      end
   end;
writeln;
writeln(m,' has maximum height of ', maxheight)
end.
```

Notes:
(1) We have employed odd(x), a boolean function provided in Pascal; this returns true if the integer x is odd, otherwise false.
(2) The repeat statement is slightly neater than a while in this application (why?), but either could be used.

(3) On some computers the program may fail with integer overflow (in that case the constant nmax should be set to some smaller value). For large enough values of nmax, the program can be made to fail on any computer (but see exercise set A).

Test run:

```
Integer <= 10000 with longest Collatz sequence ...
     Integer    Height
        3          7
        6          8
        7         16
        9         19
       18         20
       25         23
       27        111
       54        112
       73        115
       97        118
      129        121
      171        124
      231        127
      313        130
      327        143
      649        144
      703        170
      871        178
     1161        181
     2223        182
     2463        208
     2919        216
     3711        237
     6171        261

6171 has maximum height of 261
```

3.3 Input and Output

In many applications the first task to be performed by a program is to read in a set of data supplied by the user. Data may, of course, be entered from the keyboard, but this method is very inconvenient and error-prone when large data sets are involved. Instead, it is common practice to store the data in a *data file* and associate this file at runtime with the program parameter input (the specific way this is done depends on the system). It is not necessary to know in advance how many data values are present in the file; it is possible to read the data from the file under the control of a **while** statement which terminates as soon as the last value has been read in. It is for this purpose that Pascal provides the boolean function eof, which returns the value true if and only if the end of file has been reached. The following program illustrates how this works in practice.

Example 3.3

```
program StandardDeviation (input, output);
(* This program computes the mean and standard deviation of a set
   of real numbers read from a data file, one item per line.
   Note that the 'sample standard deviation' s satisfies
        s^2  =  (sum of squares - n(square of mean))/(n-1)      *)
var
   n : integer;
   x, sumx, sumsq, mean : real;
begin
n := 0;  sumx := 0;  sumsq := 0;
while not eof do
   begin     (* read data to end of file *)
   readln(x);
   n := n + 1;
   sumx  := sumx + x;
   sumsq := sumsq + sqr(x)
   end;
writeln(n:6, ' numbers in data file');
if n > 1 then
   begin     (* compute mean and standard deviation *)
   mean := sumx/n;
   writeln('   Mean = ', mean:8:4);
   writeln('   Standard deviation = ',
            sqrt((sumsq - n*sqr(mean))/(n-1)) :8:4)
   end
end.
```

Notes:
(1) We input the data with readln rather than read when using eof with a data file (this reads a value from each line, then moves to the next line). There is a technical reason why this is necessary which will be explained in section 8.3.
(2) Output statements can be used with any number of parameters - text, variables, expressions - separated by commas.
(3) To aid the programmer in producing readable output, Pascal provides a simple *format specification* which controls the layout of results. Thus n:6 causes

an integer value to be output (right-justified) in a *field* of width 6, while mean:8:4 causes a real value to be output in a field of total width 8 with 4 digits after the decimal point (remember the rule :w:d). If the digit specification is absent, say mean:10, then the real value is output in *e notation* in a field of the specified width. If a format is not specified at all, as in our earlier examples, then a default format will be used (the default depends on the Pascal implementation and is one reason why some of the output produced on your system may not be exactly the same as ours).

Test run:

With an input file containing the data

```
 1.4
 2.6
-1.8
 3.2
 4.4
-0.5
 4.9
-2.1
-0.9
 2.7
```

the results obtained are

```
10 numbers in data file
Mean =   1.3900
Standard deviation =   2.5606
```

4. Arrays

The variables we have met so far are called *simple* (believe it or not) because the value is a single number or, in the case of boolean, a truth value. In many mathematical applications we find it necessary to perform operations on objects such as vectors and matrices which consist of structured collections of values; to represent these in our programs we use variables of composite type known as *arrays*. A given array is designed to hold a set of values all of the same type, such as real or integer (in Pascal any type is allowed). Although they constitute a collective whole denoted by a single variable name, the *elements* of an array can be accessed individually in a way to be explained below.

4.1 Array Declarations

The following declarations introduce four arrays.

```
var
    x, y : array[0..100] of real;
    v    : array[-50..50] of integer;
    bvec : array[1..16] of boolean;
```

(the pairs of dots are part of the syntax). Each of the variables x, y, v, bvec is endowed with a single *subscript* (also known as an *index*) and is said to be a 1-dimensional array or, loosely, a vector. For example, x and y represent vectors with 101 real components; the *subscript range* 0..100 is specified as part of the declaration, as is the component type real. The *bounds* on the subscript, in this case 0 and 100, must be constants, not variables or expressions; although usually of type integer, these may be of any 'ordinal' type (for which see section 5.2).

The components of x can be referenced as *subscripted variables* x[0], x[1],...,x[100]. We may use an integer variable or expression as a subscript provided its value falls within the specified subscript range. This is an extremely useful feature, but we must observe the rules. The simplest case is x[i], with $0 \leq i \leq 100$. A more complicated example is x[2*i-2], which will be a valid array reference if and only if $0 \leq 2{*}i{-}2 \leq 100$, that is, $1 \leq i \leq 51$. Attempting to access a non-existent array element such as $x[101]$ is a common programming mistake which gives rise to the runtime error *array subscript out of bounds*.

Subscripted variables can be used in every respect like ordinary variables of the same type. As in the case of ordinary variables, the declaration of an array does not associate any value with it; as a consequence, array elements are undefined unless values have been assigned to them. This can be done conveniently by means of a **for** statement; for example,

```
for i := 0 to 100 do
    begin
    read(x[i]);
    y[i] := 2*x[i]
    end
```

Example 4.1

Consider if you will the array of integers

```
1
1   1
1   3   1
1   7   6   1
.   .   .   .   .
```

Each row after the first is derived in a certain way from the row above. To see how, let us take the third and fourth rows and call them 'old' and 'new' respectively; at the same time we append the column index k.

$k =$	1	2	3	4
Old	1	3	1	
New	1	7	6	1

Apart from the end elements, which are always equal to 1, the new row is obtained from the old as follows: multiply each old element by the corresponding k and add its left-hand neighbour. Thus

$$2 \times 3 + 1 = 7 \qquad 3 \times 1 + 3 = 6$$

You should be able to work out the fifth row by the same process. It is

$$1 \quad 15 \quad 25 \quad 10 \quad 1$$

The *recurrence relation* we have described can be used to generate as many rows as we wish. The integers produced are called the Stirling numbers of the second kind, and they are of interest in combinatorial problems.

How can we compute the Stirling numbers? We need a row index, say n. The following fragment then implements the recurrence relation for row n.

```
New[n] := 1;
for k := n-1 downto 2 do
   New[k] := k*Old[k] + Old[k-1]
```

Notice that the values are filled in from right to left. A little thought shows that, because of this, Old and New can be held in one and the same vector (call it S); by the time S[k] is *overwritten* with its new value, the old value is no longer required. Follow this through for the cases above to convince yourself. If the values of S[1],...,S[n] are then written out before the next iteration starts, the entire computation can be carried out using just one vector.

```
program Stirling (output);
(* This program outputs the Stirling numbers of the
   second kind of index n for n = 1,...,nmax *)
const
   nmax = 10;

var
   S    : array[1..nmax] of integer;
   k, n : integer;
begin
for n := 1 to nmax do
   begin
   S[n] := 1;
   for k := n-1 downto 2 do
      S[k] := k*S[k] + S[k-1];
   for k := 1 to n do      (* output n-th row *)
      write(S[k]:7);
   writeln
   end
end.
```

Test run:

```
1
1      1
1      3      1
1      7      6      1
1     15     25     10      1
1     31     90     65     15      1
1     63    301    350    140     21      1
1    127    966   1701   1050    266     28      1
1    255   3025   7770   6951   2646    462     36      1
1    511   9330  34105  42525  22827   5880    750     45      1
```

It is a point of style with good programmers to avoid using unnecessary storage, always provided that this does not obscure the clarity of a program. If you find that you are declaring many arrays, or arrays with a large number of elements, ask yourself if you can attain the same ends more economically and 'elegantly'. There is a limit to the amount of memory even of the largest computer, and there are problems in which economizing on storage is essential.

4.2 Array Types

The arrays we have been using are of definite types, specified in a **var** declaration, but the types have no names (unlike, say, integer or real); they are said to be *anonymous*. It is possible and quite usual to name array types in a **type** definition at the top of the program (see 'program structure' in chapter 1). This is our first example of a *user-defined type*.

```
type
    vector = array[0..100] of real;
var
    x, y : vector;   (* 'vector' is an arbitrary identifier *)
```

This has the same effect as the first declaration in section 4.1, with the added advantage that the type of x and y has a name, vector.

We can also declare arrays with two or more subscripts. The simplest way to declare a 2-dimensional array, which may be used to represent a matrix, is

```
var
    A : array[1..10, 1..20] of real;
```

This declares a real-valued array which we may think of as comprising 10 rows and 20 columns. We refer to the element in row i, column j as A[i,j] (the notation is analogous to matrix notation in mathematics). This interpretation could have been made explicit by introducing A as follows:

```
type
    row = array[1..20] of real;
var
    A : array[1..10] of row;
```

Here, each component of A is itself an array (of type row). More generally, in Pascal we may declare arrays with components of any predefined or user-defined type.

The next example illustrates the use of arrays to perform a basic and very important computation in linear algebra.

Example 4.2

```
program AxProduct (input, output);
(* This program reads an integer n <= maxsize, then the elements of
   an nxn matrix A and an n-component vector x (both real-valued)
   in the order
            A[i,1]  A[i,2]   ....   A[i,n]     x[i]
   for i = 1,...,n.
   It outputs the components of the product vector y = Ax  *)
const
   maxsize = 10;

type
   vector = array[1..maxsize] of real;
   matrix = array[1..maxsize, 1..maxsize] of real;

var
   x, y    : vector;
   A       : matrix;
   i, j, n : integer;
   sum     : real;

begin
readln(n);
if (n<1) or (n>maxsize) then
   writeln(n, ' is not acceptable as an array bound')
else
   begin
   (* Read in the data *)
   for i := 1 to n do
      begin
      for j := 1 to n do
         read(A[i,j]);
      readln(x[i])
      end;

   (* Calculate the product Ax
      and assign result to vector y *)
   for i := 1 to n do
      begin
      sum := 0;
      for j := 1 to n do
         sum := sum + A[i,j]*x[j];
      y[i] := sum
      end;
```

```
   (* Output the result *)
   writeln;  writeln('Product vector is:');
   for i := 1 to n do
      writeln(y[i]:10)
   end
end.
```

Test run:

The input is conveniently read from a data file.

```
3
3   -1.5    6      1.2
9    3     -3     -5.6
3    6    -15     -2.0
```

```
Product vector is:
-1.776e-15
 1.776e-15
 7.105e-15
```

The vector x 'happens' to be a solution of the system of equations $Ax = 0$ (check), so all the components of y should be 0. According to our computer none are; the nonzero values for the components are due solely to *rounding errors* arising from the finite precision of the machine. The exact results are *machine-dependent*.

4.3 Subrange Types

In example 4.2 we have used subscript variables i, j of type integer. However, the subscripts can only sensibly take on values in a subrange 1..maxsize of integer. Pascal allows us to define *subrange data types* and use these, for example, to specify subscript types:

```
type
    index  = 1..maxsize;   (* a subrange of integer *)
    vector = array[index] of real;
    matrix = array[index, index] of real;
```

Then if the variables i and j are declared as

```
var
    i, j : index;
```

any (erroneous) attempt to set i or j to values lying outside the subrange 1..maxsize will be detected immediately as an error by the Pascal system.

Example 4.3

Here is a game for a rainy Sunday afternoon: starting with a list of integers 1,2,3,4,5, ..., n, we cross out every second number to obtain the sequence of odd integers 1,3,5, ... From this we cross out every third number, and from the resulting list every fourth number, and so on. Any integer that is never crossed out when this process is applied exhaustively is said to be a 'Sunday number'. Today is not a Sunday, so let us save time by writing a program which will output the Sunday numbers less than or equal to a specified integer *n*.

```pascal
program SundayList (input, output);
(* This program outputs the 'Sunday numbers' <= n,
   where n (<=nmax) is read in as data  *)
const
    nmax     = 1000;
    halfmax  =  500;

type
    range     = 1..nmax;
    halfrange = 1..halfmax;
    vector    = array[halfrange] of range;
var
    j, n : range;
    i, s : halfrange;
    list : vector;

begin
writeln;
writeln('List of Sunday numbers <= n');
write('Enter n (<=', nmax:4, ') :   ');
readln(n);  (* the value entered for n must be of type range *)

(* Start with list of odd integers *)
n := (n+1) div 2;
for i := 1 to n do
   list[i] := 2*i-1;

(* For s = 3,4,... delete every s-th number
   and close up the gaps *)
s := 3;
while s<=n do
   begin
   i := s; j := s+1;
   while j<=n do
      begin
      list[i] := list[j];
      i := i+1;   j := j+1;
```

```
        if j mod s = 0 then j := j+1
        end;
   n := i-1;
   s := s+1
   end;
(* Output list of 'survivors' *)
writeln;
for i := 1 to n do
   write(list[i]:4);
writeln
end.
```

Test run:

```
List of Sunday numbers <= n
Enter n (<=1000) :  1000

   1   3   7  13  19  27  39  49  63  79  91 109 133 147 181 207
 223 253 289 307 349 387 399 459 481 529 567 613 649 709 763 807
 843 927 949
```

5. Functions

The programming examples presented so far have been mostly short and very simple. This is not at all characteristic of real-life programs, which are more complicated and usually much longer. Designing such programs would be extremely difficult and error-prone if it were not possible to break down the problem, and hence the program, into smaller, self-contained components capable of being developed and tested separately, to be combined at a later stage. Such program units in Pascal are known as *subprograms*. A subprogram may be either a *function* or a *procedure*. In the present chapter we shall discuss Pascal functions; procedures will be introduced in chapter 6.

5.1 Predeclared Functions

We have already met *predeclared functions* (e.g. sin, sqr, sqrt). These can be used in Pascal as though they were part of the language, although they actually represent subprograms that have been written to perform the necessary computations. A function is *called* by writing its name with an argument of appropriate type. If and when execution reaches that part of the program, the function computes a value of specified type which can be used like any other value in Pascal.

```
x := sqrt(11.7);
y := 1.5 - sin(sqr(x+2.1));
write(sin(x), sqr(y));
etc.
```

The predeclared functions in the following list are basically mathematical and their use is fairly obvious. Two of these, unlike most functions, can take arguments which may be either real or integer (referred to here as 'arithmetic types').

```
function abs (x : any arithmetic type) : same type;
```
returns the absolute value of x

```
function arctan (x : real) : real;
```
computes the inverse tangent (in radians) of x

```
function cos (x : real) : real;
```
computes the cosine of angle x (expressed in radians)

```
function exp (x : real) : real;
```
computes e^x

```
function ln (x : real) : real;
```
computes the logarithm to base e of x

```
function odd (x : integer) : boolean;
```
returns `true` if the integer x is odd , otherwise `false`

```
function round (x : real) : integer;
```
returns x rounded to the nearest integer

```
function sin (x : real) : real;
```
computes the sine of angle x (expressed in radians)

```
function sqr (x : any arithmetic type) : same type;
```
returns the square of x

```
function sqrt (x : real) : real;
```
computes the square root of x

```
function trunc (x : real) : integer;
```
returns x truncated to its integral part

There are a few other predeclared functions available in Pascal. These include `chr`, which refers to data type `char` (to be introduced in chapter 7), and `eof` and `eoln`, which are file handling functions whose purpose is explained in some detail in chapter 8. In addition there are three functions associated with so-called ordinal types; these functions are used particularly in the special case of enumerated types, which will be explained next.

5.2 Enumerated Types

In Pascal one can define a data type by *enumerating* (explicitly listing) the elements which are to constitute the type. An example often given is the collection of days of the week: Sunday, Monday, ..., Saturday. By means of a type definition we can make this into an *enumerated type*:

```
type
    day = (Sunday, Monday, Tuesday, Wednesday, Thursday,
                    Friday, Saturday);
```

We may then declare variables of type day,

```
var
    today, tomorrow : day;
```

and proceed to make assignments and comparisons,

```
today := Wednesday;  tomorrow := succ(today);  (* see below *)
if tomorrow = Sunday then ...
```

Like integer types, and also type char (chapter 7), enumerated types are *ordinal*, the order being implied by the list in the type definition. The predeclared function

```
function ord (x : any ordinal type) : integer;
```

returns the ordinal number of the element x, where the first element in the list has ordinal number 0. Thus, with the type definition above,

```
ord(Thursday) = 4
```

If the type is integer, the ordinal number is the value of the integer itself:

```
ord(10) = 10      ord (-10) = -10
```

We also remark that type boolean is a predefined enumerated type,

```
boolean = (false, true);
```

hence ord(false) = 0, while the boolean expression false < true has the value true!

There are two extra functions defined on any ordinal type, the *successor* and *predecessor* functions, which yield the immediate successor and predecessor respectively. These are available as two predeclared functions,

```
function succ (x : any ordinal type) : same type;
function pred (x : any ordinal type) : same type;
```

Since the last element in a list has no successor, succ is not defined for such elements, and its use in this case would give rise to an error; a similar caveat applies to the predecessor of the first element.

It should be clear that enumerated types are a disguised form of subranges of integer; their main use is to enhance the readability of certain programs.

5.3 User-declared Functions

A programmer can augment the repertoire of available functions by making up his or her own. Such *user-declared functions*, unlike predeclared functions, have to be defined by the programmer before they can be used. This is done by

means of a *function declaration*, which consists of two parts:
(1) a *function heading* specifying the name of the function, the arguments (*formal parameters*) with their types and the type of the result, and
(2) a *function block* comprising any *local declarations* and a compound statement to work out the desired function value. A function declaration therefore takes the form

```
function name (list of parameters, if any, with types)
              : type of function value;
    Declaration of any 'local' constants, types, variables etc;
    begin
    statements to work out the function value
    end;
```

Example 5.1
To illustrate the basic idea we give some examples of function declarations.

```
function tan (x : real) : real;
(* Computes the tangent of angle x (expressed in radians) *)
    begin
    tan := sin(x)/cos(x)
    end;

function area (a, b, c : real) : real;
(* Computes the area of a triangle, given the three sides *)
    var
        s : real;    (* local variable *)
    begin
    s := (a+b+c)/2;
    area := sqrt(s*(s-a)*(s-b)*(s-c))
    end (* area *);

function max (x, y : integer) : integer;
(* Returns the larger of the two integer arguments *)
    begin
    if x > y then
        max := x
    else
        max := y
    end (* max *);
```

Notes:
(1) The function must contain at least one statement assigning a value of appropriate type to the function name; this is how the result is returned. The name of the function should not appear on the right hand side of any assignment statement in the function body; if it does, this has a special significance to be discussed in chapter 9.

(2) Local objects such as variable s in function area come into existence only when the function is activated and persist only as long as the function is being executed. They have no meaning outside the subprogram. For example, a program making use of function area might have a variable (or constant, or array) called s; this would have no connection whatever with the local variable s.

(3) A function may itself contain a function declaration which will then be local to it in the above sense. In principle, 'nesting' to any depth is possible, but in the interests of clarity this is not to be encouraged.

(4) The parameters of a function may be of any Pascal type, and may include subprograms (for an example see section 13.1). The value returned by a function must be of a *simple* type (for our purposes, real or ordinal). Composite values such as arrays cannot be returned as function values.

Example 5.2

We conclude with a more ambitious application to illustrate the preceding ideas. Pascal does not provide an operator or a predeclared function for powers, apart from sqr; we write our own function to compute x^n, where x is real and n is integer (the following is not the most efficient method of computing powers, but for fairly small values of n it is acceptable).

```
function Power (x : real;  n : integer) : real;
(* Computes x to the power n, where n is any integer.
   NOTE: this function returns the value 0 if the power
   is undefined, i.e. when x=0 and n<=0 *)
   var
       i : integer;   (* local variable *)
       p : real;      (* local variable *)
   begin
   if x = 0 then
      Power := 0
   else
      begin      (* check for n negative *)
      if n < 0 then
         begin
         x := 1/x;  n := abs(n)
         end;
      (* Compute x^n by multiplication *)
      p := 1;
      for i := 1 to n do
         p := p*x;
      Power := p
      end
   end (* Power *);
```

We shall use this to tabulate the function

$$f(x) \;=\; \frac{(1-x)^3 x^4}{(1+x)^5}$$

for $x = 0.0,\ 0.2,\ \ldots,\ 1.0$.

```pascal
program Tabulate (input, output);
(* This program tabulates function f(x) below over a range of x.
   The initial argument, step size and number of tabulation points
   are read in as data *)

var
   x, x0, step : real;
   i, n        : integer;

<function Power declared here>

function f (x : real) : real;
   begin
   f := Power(1-x,3) * Power(x,4) * Power(1+x,-5)
   end;

begin   (* main program *)
writeln;
writeln('Tabulation of f(x) ...');
writeln;
write('Enter initial value of x:  '); readln(x0);
write('Enter step size and number of points:  '); readln(step, n);
writeln;
writeln('     x           f(x)');   (* table heading *)
writeln;
for i := 0 to n-1 do
   begin
   x := x0 + i*step;
   write('   ', x:5:2);  writeln('    ', f(x):10)
   end
end.
```

Notes:

(1) The function declarations come after the var section of the main program; Power must appear before f, which calls it.

(2) Power is called three times; the arguments or *actual parameters* - which may be constants, variables or expressions of appropriate type - are respectively

1-x,	3	first call
x,	4	second call
1+x,	-5	third call

(3) When function `Power` is activated, the values of the *actual parameters* above are assigned as the initial values of the corresponding *formal parameters* x and n in the function. This is a *one-way process*: the formal parameters are local to the function block. Even if an actual parameter happens to be a variable (such as x in the second call), its value in the calling program remains unaffected by any operations performed inside the function body (e.g. x := 1/x in our example).

(4)   The local variable i in function `Power` and the variable i in the main program are completely different entities with no connection whatever.

Test run:

```
Tabulation of f(x) ...

Enter initial value of x:  0.0
Enter step size and number of points:  0.2   6
      x        f(x)
    0.00     0.000e+00
    0.20     3.292e-04
    0.40     1.028e-03
    0.60     7.910e-04
    0.80     1.734e-04
    1.00     0.000e+00
```

6. Procedures

As we have seen in chapter 5, a Pascal function is a self-contained program module which is capable of being used in many different programs. For a given list of actual parameters, it computes a single value of some 'simple' type. Yet there are many cases where we would like a subprogram to return more than one value or a result of some composite type such as an array. In other situations we may want a subprogram to perform tasks such as displaying data or drawing a graph without necessarily returning any values. In such cases a function would be unsuitable; instead, we use the more general form of subprogram known as a *procedure*.

We have already met the predeclared Pascal procedures read and write. Like some of the predeclared functions, these are irregular in that the types of the parameters can vary and not even the number of parameters is fixed. There are several other predeclared procedures, some of which will be introduced in chapter 8. In the present chapter we shall learn how to declare and use our own procedures. Intelligent use of procedures and functions can make the high-level structure of a program more transparent - the interrelationship of its parts is clearer, easier to understand and less susceptible to logical mistakes.

6.1 User-declared Procedures

A procedure is declared in a similar way to a function except that no type is provided for it and no value is assigned to the procedure name:

```
procedure name (list of parameters, if any, with types);
    Declaration of any local constants, types, variables etc;
    begin
    Body of procedure
    end;
```

The procedure is called simply by writing its name followed by a list of actual parameters corresponding to the formal parameters of the declaration. Any results are returned to the calling program or subprogram via the parameter list. This is done by the use of so-called **var** parameters in a way to be explained next.

Example 6.1

```
procedure maxmin (n : integer; var x : vector;
                  var xmax, xmin : real);
(* This procedure finds the largest and (algebraically) smallest
   of the vector components x[1],...,x[n]. It returns the two
   values in xmax and xmin. Note the use of the data type
   'vector'; this would be defined in the calling program
   as something like
            vector = array[1..m] of real
   where m is a constant >= n   *)

var
   i : integer;    (* local variable *)

begin
xmax := x[1];    xmin := x[1];
for i := 2 to n do
   if x[i] > xmax then
       xmax := x[i]
   else if x[i] < xmin then
       xmin := x[i]
end (* maxmin *);
```

A possible call of this procedure might be

```
maxmin(100, v, x, y)
```

In the calling program, v would be an array of type vector and x and y two real variables (there is no requirement for actual parameters to have the same names as formal parameters, and in fact no connection is implied by the names). Any values that x and y might have had will be replaced as a result of the procedure activation by the values of the largest and smallest components of the vector v. This is because the corresponding formal parameters xmax and xmin appear in the parameter list of maxmin as **var** parameters. In simple terms, any change made to a var parameter in the subprogram body *changes the value of the corresponding actual parameter* (which must therefore be a variable, not a constant or an expression). This is how results are passed out of the procedure. The mechanism is termed *call-by-reference*: instead of the *value* of the actual parameter, its *address* or memory location is passed to the subprogram and this is used for returning the results.

Note that the formal parameter x of maxmin is quoted as a **var** parameter even though it serves only for input to the procedure and none of its components are changed in any way by the computation. The reason for this is that calling arrays 'by value' is inefficient and uneconomical; a local copy would have to be created when the subprogram was activated, and in the case of large structures this carries overheads and is a waste of valuable storage.

If a formal parameter is not qualified as a **var** parameter (as is the case with n in our example), then by default it is *called by value*. This is the most appropriate mechanism for functions and is the only one used in chapter 5. Functions are not normally expected to change the values of their arguments (such changes are called *side-effects* and are usually unintended and highly undesirable). However, even in the case of functions, parameters of composite type such as arrays can and should be called by reference, for the reasons explained above.

6.2 A Complete Program

To illustrate the ideas of section 6.1, we present a complete program containing a procedure to solve quadratic equations by the well-known formula.

Example 6.2

```
program Quad (input, output);
(* This program computes the real roots (if any) of a quadratic
   equation, obtaining them by procedure QuadSolve below. It can
   handle the degenerate case of a linear equation, but complex
   roots are not attempted - a message is output instead.
   The user is prompted to enter the three coefficients of the
   equation at the keyboard and is offered repeat runs *)

var
   a, b, c, x, y : real;
   n             : integer;
   again         : char;   (* a character variable - see chapter 7 *)

procedure QuadSolve
              (a, b, c : real;    (* coefficients of quadratic      *)
          var x1, x2 : real;    (* real roots returned via these *)
          var count  : integer (* number of roots / indicator   *)
                    );
(* This procedure computes any real roots of the quadratic equation
          a*x^2 + b*x + c = 0
```

returning them in x1 and x2. If the equation is linear, a single
root is returned in x1. The indicator count is returned as 1 or 2
for real roots, 0 if there are no roots, -1 if roots are complex *)

```
var
    t : real;   (* local variable *)
begin
if a=0 then
    if b=0 then
       count := 0   (* no roots *)
    else
       begin   (* equation is linear *)
       count := 1;   x1 := -c/b
       end
else
    begin   (* a non-degenerate quadratic *)
    t := sqr(b) - 4*a*c;
    if t < 0 then
       count := -1   (* roots are complex *)
    else
       begin   (* roots are real *)
       count := 2;
       t := sqrt(t);
       if b < 0 then
          x1 := (-b+t)/(2*a)
       else
          x1 := (-b-t)/(2*a);
       (* There is a numerical reason for doing this, to avoid
          'cancellation error' if |b| and t are nearly equal
          (see section 14.2). The remaining root is found as:   *)
       if x1 = 0 then
          x2 := 0
       else
          x2 := c/(a*x1)
       end
    end
end (* QuadSolve *);

begin   (* main program *)
writeln;
writeln('Solving quadratic equations ...');
writeln;
repeat
    write('Enter coefficients  a  b  c :  ');
    readln(a, b, c);
    QuadSolve(a, b, c, x, y, n);     (* procedure call! *)
```

```
  case n of
    -1:  writeln('Roots are complex');
     0:  writeln('Equation has no roots');
     1:  writeln('Equation linear, one root:  ', x:10);
     2:  writeln('Two real roots:  ', x:10, '  ', y:10)
    end (* case *);
  writeln;
  repeat
    write('Another go, y or n?  ');
    readln(again)
  until (again = 'y') or (again = 'n')
until again = 'n'
end.
```

Note:

In the main program above we make a multiple selection by means of a **case** statement, which is a neat alternative to multiple **if** tests:

```
        case n of
          -1:  ............ ;
           0:  ............ ;
           1:  ............ ;
           2:  ............
          end;
```

The possible values of the *selector* n appear as *case labels* −1, 0, 1, 2, each followed by a colon, then a statement. Depending on the value of n, exactly one of these statements is selected and the rest ignored. There must be a case label for every possible value of the selector, otherwise a runtime error may result. Several labels, separated by commas, may be attached to any statement. The statements may be compound or even empty.

Test run:

```
Solving quadratic equations ...

Enter coefficients  a  b  c :  1  1 -2
Two real roots:  -2.000e+00    1.000e+00

Another go, y or n?  y
Enter coefficients  a  b  c :  0  2  3
Equation linear, one root:  -1.500e+00

Another go, y or n?  y
Enter coefficients  a  b  c :  1  0  1
Roots are complex

Another go, y or n?  n
```

6.3 Blocks and Scope

Pascal is called a *block-structured* language. This means that procedures and functions can be nested to any depth, and objects (variables, constants etc.) can be declared and redeclared at the various levels. We discourage the use of deeply nested structuring as this tends to obscure the logic of a program and may give rise to tricky situations that many programmers find difficult to cope with. However, an acquaintance with the rules governing the *visibility* of objects within blocks (that is, the *scope* of their declarations) is in order. Even if we declare just a single procedure and one or two local functions, it is not immediately obvious what happens, for example, when an identifier in an embracing block is redeclared in one of the inner blocks. We state a few basic rules and illustrate them with an example.

(1) Any constant, type or variable identifier declared in the main program is visible and can be accessed within a particular subprogram, provided the identifier does not appear in a local declaration or as a formal parameter. Such objects are said to be *global*. Similarly, with the same proviso, the scope of objects declared in a subprogram extends to any locally-declared subprograms (the objects are said to be *non-local* to the latter). However, in standard Pascal a non-local variable cannot be used as the control variable in a **for** statement (although some non-standard compilers may allow this).

(2)   If a global or non-local variable is assigned a value, this value takes effect in the surrounding blocks up to the level where the variable was declared. This is a *side-effect* which can have unexpected and confusing results in a program; it should be avoided.

(3)   When an identifier is redeclared in an inner block, the original object of the same name becomes inaccessible - it is temporarily *out of scope* - but retains its value or meaning until it is again visible. We say that there is a *hole in the scope* of such an identifier.

Example 6.3

```
program Obscure (output);
const
   nmax = 100;
type
   range = 1..nmax;
   vec   = array[range] of real;
var
   m, n, c : integer;
```

```
function f (n : integer) : integer;
   const
       nmax = 10;
   type
       range = 0..nmax;
   var
       i   : range;
       vec : array[range] of integer;
   begin    (* body of function f *)
   writeln('c = ', c);
   for i := 0 to nmax do vec[i] := m*i;
   f := n*vec[nmax]
   end (* f *);

procedure proc;
   var
       c : range;
   begin    (* body of procedure proc *)
   c := 50;    m := f(c) + 1
   end (* proc *);

begin    (* main program  *)
m := 3;   c := 5;
n := f(nmax);   proc;
writeln('m = ', m)
end.
```

Notes:

(1) The identifiers nmax, range, vec and n which are declared at the top of the program are redeclared in function f and are therefore not visible within this function (their scope has a hole). Variables c and m are global to f and hence their values will be those which are assigned to them in the main program. See if you can work out the value of n after the function call f(nmax).

(2) Procedure proc does not redeclare range, so this identifier refers to the type definition made at the start of the program. Variable c is declared as local to proc and is assigned the value 50. Now when f is called from within proc, what is the value of c that will be output?

(3) Variable m is global to both f and proc. The value 3 is assigned to it at the start of the main program and is not changed by any statement appearing in the program body. Yet when we print the value of m (in the last line) it will not be 3. This is because the value has been changed as a side-effect when procedure proc was activated. (Can you work out the value without running the program?) As you can see, a side-effect can have puzzling consequences which are not always easy to account for, since the source may be difficult to spot in a larger program. You should not write programs like this!

Exercise Set A

1.1 The formula for the sum $1^2 + 2^2 + \ldots + n^2$ is $n(n+1)(2n+1)/6$. Modify program Sum (example 1.1) to output this along with the other values. Note the different form of output produced in this case. The reason is explained at the end of section 2.1. Read this, and see if you can make the program produce a true integer value.

1.2 Modify program Rectangle (example 1.2) to compute approximations to

$$\int_1^2 (1 - x)\,dx\,, \quad \int_0^3 x^2\,dx\,, \quad \int_0^{10} (1 + x^2)^{-1}\,dx\,, \quad \int_0^{\pi/2} \sin x\,dx$$

(note that pi is not a 'predefined' constant in Pascal, i.e. its value is not known to the system). Which of the results is exactly correct? Can you account for this?

1.3 The area of a triangle with sides of length a, b, c is given by the formula $[s(s - a)(s - b)(s - c)]^{1/2}$, where $s = (a + b + c)/2$. Write two assignment statements to compute the area (the Pascal function for square root is sqrt). Develop a program with a, b and c as real constants and a write statement to output the area. Check that the results are correct in some known cases (3, 4, 5; 5, 5, 6; 5, 12, 13). Try the program out on some other triangles - what happens if a 'triangle' has one side longer than the sum of the other two sides?

2.1 Find out if your Pascal system gives a runtime failure on integer overflow; if not, what does it do with the integer value maxint + 1? (You may need some ingenuity to get this past the compiler.) Also check that (a div b)*b + a mod b = a for a $\geq$ 0 and b > 0 (what happens if a or b are negative?)

2.2 As well as a maximum real number representable on the computer, there is also a minimum positive real number (if we call this minreal, then the only real number that the computer can represent between minreal and -minreal is 0.0). Modify program MaxReal (section 2.3) to find an approximation to the minimum positive real number (consider using a while statement as in example 2.2: while x > 0 do ...).

2.3 Modify program ImprovedIntegral (example 2.2) to compute an approximation to $\int_0^{\pi/2}\sin x\,dx$ $-$ 1. What should the exact answer be? Execute the program for n = 10, 20, 40, 80. See if you can conjecture from the results how the error of the composite rectangle rule depends on the step size (what happens, approximately, when n is doubled?)

2.4 Write a program fragment using a for statement to compute k^m by repeated multiplication, where k and m are positive integers. Make this into a compound statement and incorporate it in an outer for loop to calculate the sum of the mth powers of the first n integers, $1^m + 2^m + \ldots + n^m$. (You should now have what is known as a 'nested' for loop.) Finally, develop a program with n and m as constants and a write statement to output the sum. Check that the results are correct for some small values of n and m.

3.1 Modify the program of example 3.1 to output the truth table for a boolean expression of four variables. Execute on

   (r or s) or (p and not q) or (not r and p) or not (s and not q)

This expression is a tautology, i.e. it has the value true in all cases.

3.2 Write a program to output the Collatz sequence (see example 3.2) for any positive integer n; the program should also record and output the largest integer generated. Check the results for n = 3, 4, 5, 6, then execute on n = 6171. Try the program again with n = 113383, *but limit the number of iterations to 1000*. If your system checks for integer overflow (see exercise 2.1), execution will stop with an error message; otherwise negative terms will be generated until all 1000 iterations have been used up.

3.3 Let *base* be a fixed integer > 1 (for the purpose of this exercise we shall assume that *base* is also even). Any non-negative integer n can be written uniquely in the form $n = n1 \times base + n0$, where $0 \le n0 < base$. Thus each n is characterized by a pair $(n1, n0)$. For given $n1$ and $n0$, write three assignment statements (using the operators div and mod) to work out the pair corresponding to the integer $3n$. Similarly, assuming that n is even, write a program fragment to determine the pair that represents the integer $n/2$.

3.4 Taking maxint div 3 as the value of *base*, incorporate the code of the last exercise into program Collatz, representing all the terms of the sequences in 'pair' form. Execute the program and check the results. Now attempt to output the Collatz sequence for n = 113383 (see exercise 3.2); this time the program should not fail even though the largest intermediate number is 2482111348.

3.5 Write a program to compute the root mean square $(\Sigma x_i^2 / n)^{1/2}$ of a set of real numbers read from a data file. Check that correct results are produced for some small data sets, then execute on the data of example 3.3.

4.1 *Pascal's triangle* is the array

```
1
1  1
1  2  1
1  3  3  1
.  .  .  .  .
```

These integers are the binomial coefficients, i.e. the coefficients appearing in the expansion of $(1 + x)^n$ for $n = 0, 1, 2, 3, \ldots$. Write a program to output the first ten rows of Pascal's triangle.

4.2 Modify program AxProduct to compute:
(1) the inner (scalar) product of two vectors;
(2) the matrix product of two $n \times n$ matrices.
Check the correctness for some simple cases with $n = 2, 3$, then try some larger examples.

4.3 An integer p greater than 1 is said to be a *prime number* if it is divisible only by 1 and p. The sequence of prime numbers starts with 2, 3, 5, 7, 11, ... Write a program to determine the first 100 primes (by checking each candidate in turn, with any short cuts you can think of), storing the results in a vector and then outputting them. Modify your program so that the user can ask for just the kth prime number to be output. A suitable message should be displayed if the value entered for k is greater than 100 or less than 1.

5.1 Write a Pascal function sign (x : real) : integer which returns 1 if x is positive, 0 if x is zero and −1 if x is negative. Devise a method using sign to locate a value of x that satisfies the equation $x^3 - c = 0$, where c is a constant between 0 and 1. Hence compute $0.5^{1/3}$ correct to 2 decimal places. Repeat the exercise to find an approximate solution of the equation $x + \log_e x = 0$.

5.2 The *Bessel function of order* 0 may be defined by the following definite integral: $J_0(x) = \frac{1}{\pi} \int_0^\pi \cos (x \sin t) \, dt$. Using the code of example 2.2, suitably modified and with n set to 100, declare a Pascal function J0 (x : real) : real to compute an approximation to $J_0(x)$. The integrand cos $(x \sin t)$ is conveniently specified as a function local to J0. Develop a program to tabulate the values of $J_0(x)$ and $(J_0(x))^2 - J_0(x^2)$ over the range $x = 0 \, (0.1) \, 2$.

6.1 Modify procedure QuadSolve to compute complex as well as real roots. (You do not need complex numbers for this; if the root is $x + iy$, you could use the parameters x1 and x2 to return the real numbers x and y.) Arrange for suitable output in the main program, and test on as representative a range of equations as possible.

6.2 Let $x = x_k x_{k-1} \ldots x_0$ be a non-negative integer of $k+1$ digits. The digits x_i can be stored in a vector x of type array[-1..nmax], with k held in x[-1]. Write a simple procedure output(x) to output the digits stored in x. Next, write a procedure multiply(x, m) to multiply the integer corresponding to x by a non-negative integer m, returning the result in x. Incorporate the two procedures in a program to compute and output $n! = 1 \times 2 \times \ldots \times n$ for all values of $n \leq 100$.

6.3 The write procedure of your Pascal system has developed a fault and can output only single digits. A new write procedure has to be written which is capable of outputting any positive integer $\leq$ maxint. Suppose that you wish to output 67325. This can be visualized as outputting 6732, then printing the single digit 5 (but only the last part can be done directly!). In general, a procedure to output n might be defined as follows.

> *Output* (n) :
> if $n > 0$ then
> $\left\{ \begin{array}{l} Output\ (\ n \text{ div } 10\ ) \\ \text{print the single digit } n \text{ mod } 10 \end{array} \right.$

Implement this method as a procedure newrite(n : integer). This should itself contain a call of newrite; it is your first example of a *recursive* procedure (to be discussed in chapter 9). Explore what the procedure will do when you replace the 10 by 2 (or any integer in between).

Part 2

More Advanced Features of Pascal

7. Character Handling

7.1 Data Type Char

In addition to `integer`, `real` and `boolean`, there is another basic data type of Pascal: `char`. We can define constants and declare variables to be of type `char`, and these then represent *characters*. The set of characters available includes letters (capital and lower-case), digits (0..9), punctuation marks (comma, full stop etc), mathematical symbols (+, − etc), and blank (space).

A `char` *constant* is any character enclosed in single quotes (the quote character itself is the only exception: it must be doubled to avoid ambiguity). Thus

```
const
    comma = ',';
    stop  = '.';
    quote = '''';        (* a single quote or apostrophe *)
```

A `char` *variable* is declared as

```
var
    x : char;
```

It is possible to input single characters (`read(x)` - the data may be `9 a +` etc), output characters (`write(x)`, where the value of x may be `'9'`, `'a'`, `'+'` etc), effect assignments (`x := '*'`) and make comparisons (`if x = comma then ...`).

The computer represents characters by encoding them as positive integers. Thus it makes sense to ask if one character is 'less than' another (the boolean expression `'a' < 'z'` has the value `true`). In Pascal we normally do not need to concern ourselves with the details of the representation; there are two predeclared functions (the first of which we have met in chapter 5),

```
ord (x : char) : integer
```

and its inverse

```
chr (i : integer) : char
```

which perform the requisite conversions between the character set and the integer code values. The actual values depend on the convention used by the computer system. The most widely used such convention is ASCII (American Standard Code for Information Interchange) in which

```
ord('A') =  65 ..... ord('Z') =  90
chr(65)  = 'A' ..... chr(90)  = 'Z'

ord('a') =  97 ..... ord('z') = 122
chr(97)  = 'a' ..... chr(122) = 'z'

chr(32)  = ' ' ..... chr(42)  = '*'  etc.
```

Indeed, any integer in the range 0 to 127 corresponds to some character (on most computers this range extends to 255). Those with ASCII codes less than 32 are *control characters* (e.g. chr(7) is the 'bell character'); such characters cannot normally be input but can be output.

In text processing it is often required to convert an alphabetic character from lower into upper case or vice versa. Such conversions are easy to perform thanks to the following useful property of the character representation: the difference between all lower-case letters and their upper-case mates is constant. In order to convert a lower-case letter (say the value of a char variable ch) to the equivalent capital, it is only necessary to add the constant increment ord('A')-ord('a') on to ord(ch), then convert the resulting integer back into a character by function chr:

```
chr (ord(ch)+ord('A')-ord('a'))
```

You might check that this works for the ASCII values above.

You should now find that you can understand the following program.

Example 7.1

```
program TextChange (input, output);
(* This program reads two lines of text of total length not more
   than maxlength characters, the first line terminated by a comma,
   the second by a full stop. Output consists of the first line in
   reverse order and the second line with all lower-case letters
   converted to capitals. This is not a program of wide utility!
   In the next chapter we shall see how to read, write and manipulate
   arbitrary segments of text *)
const
   maxlength = 200;    (* maximum length of text *)
   comma = ',';        (* character constant *)
   stop  = '.';        (* character constant *)
```

```
type
   range = 0..maxlength;   (* subrange of integer *)

var
   i, end1, end2 : range;
   x : array[range] of char;  (* character vector *)

function Cap (ch : char) : char;
(* Converts a lower-case letter to the corresponding capital,
   returns any other character unchanged *)

   begin
   if ('a' <= ch) and (ch <= 'z') then   (* lower-case letter *)
      Cap := chr (ord(ch)+ord('A')-ord('a'))
   else
      Cap := ch
   end (* Cap *);

begin (* main program *)
writeln;
writeln('Type two lines of text, the first terminated by a comma,');
writeln('the second by a full stop:');
writeln;

i := 0;
repeat
   i := i+1;
   read(x[i])
until x[i] = comma;
end1 := i;
readln;      (* ready to start reading second line *)
repeat
   i := i+1;
   read(x[i])
until x[i] = stop;
end2 := i;

writeln;
x[0] := comma;
for i := end1-1 downto 0 do
   write(x[i]);
writeln;         (* start second line *)
for i := end1+1 to end2 do   (* convert to capitals *)
   write(Cap(x[i]));
writeln
end.
```

Test runs:

```
Type two lines of text, the first terminated by a comma,
the second by a full stop:
```
<u>able was I ere I saw elba,</u>
<u>   - N. Bonaparte.</u>
```
able was I ere I saw elba,
   - N.
```

[What happened here?]

```
Type two lines of text, the first terminated by a comma,
the second by a full stop:
```
<u>bmal elttil a dah yraM,</u>
<u>Her Mama had a fit.</u>
```
Mary had a little lamb,
HER MAMA HAD A FIT.
```

7.2 Character Strings

We have used strings already in `write` statements, but string types also enjoy an independent existence as a kind of generalization of `char`. We can define constants, declare variables and even make assignments and comparisons, all with reference to strings.

A string *constant* is any sequence of characters delimited by single quotes (for the reason noted earlier, a quote or apostrophe occurring within a string must be doubled). Thus

```
const
    fallacy  = ' ''Strings are hard!''';
    question = 'what''s up doc?''';
```
A string *variable* may be declared as

```
var
    t : packed array[1..20] of char;
```
or
```
type
    shortstring = packed array[1..5] of char;
var
    s : shortstring;
```

The significance of **packed** is that string values are normally represented in the computer in a compact form which need not concern us. We note, however, two points.

(1) **packed array**[1..n] **of** char and **array**[1..n] **of** char, where n is a constant > 1, are entirely distinct data types; the first represents strings of length n while the second represents n-component vectors with character-valued elements.

(2) In Pascal the exact length of a string is important, and extra blanks are commonly used as padding. In the **const** definition above, fallacy has the implied type **packed array**[1..20] **of** char (count it), while question has type **packed array**[1..15] **of** char.

It is possible to make assignments to string variables provided the assigned value is of the appropriate string type. With the declarations above,

        s := '''Eh, ';   t := fallacy

are both valid assignments, whereas s := fallacy or t := '''Eh, ' would fail because the string types are not in agreement.

String constants and variables may be supplied as arguments to write. For example,

        write(s, question, t)

would result in the output

        'Eh, what's up doc?' 'Strings are hard!'

On the other hand, strings can only be input by reading their constituent characters; the 'statement' read(s), convenient though it might be, cannot be used to input a string constant and assign it as the value of s.

7.3 Sorting

This is a problem which arises very often in computer applications. Given a list L[1..n] of 'keys' (which we may think of as arbitrary integers), we are interested in a rearrangement of the keys into non-decreasing order: we require that

$$L[i] \leq L[i+1] \quad \text{for } 1 \leq i \leq n-1$$

There are many algorithms that can solve the sorting problem in $O(n^2)$ operations, i.e. the amount of work is approximately proportional to n^2 for large n. Some methods can do better and only require $O(n \log n)$ operations; these are more efficient especially when n is large, but they are also more complicated and usually difficult to understand. We describe one of the simplest algorithms.

Insertion Sort Algorithm

Suppose we have a list L whose elements are in non-decreasing order (initially L might consist of a single element). Given a new element, key, we can include this in the list simply by locating the position in L where key must be inserted so as to preserve the ordering; the elements greater than key must then be shifted to the right to make room for it. Locating and shifting are combined for reasons of efficiency.

Here is a program fragment to sort an already existing list L[1..n] by this method. You are recommended to follow it through by hand, performing exactly the steps that the computer would. This can be a very instructive exercise which will often reveal programming mistakes. Use the algorithm to sort the list 3 2 1.

```
(* insert is a boolean variable *)
for i := 2 to n do
    begin
    key := L[i] ; j := i;
    repeat
        if key >= L[j-1] then
            insert := true     (* found the spot - position j *)
        else
            begin  (* shift element j-1 right one place *)
            L[j] := L[j-1];
            j := j-1;
            insert := (j=1)     (* reached the left end? *)
            end
    until insert;
    L[j] := key     (* insert it! *)
    end
```

This algorithm can be simplified by eliminating boolean variable insert. There would be no need for such a variable if we could be sure that key is always inserted before the left end of the list is reached or, put differently, if key is never inserted in the leftmost position. Such a situation can be created artificially if we introduce a so-called *stopper element* or *sentinel* as list element L[0] and assign to it a value which is known to be less than any of the bona fide list elements. If these are integers, then a suitable value would be -maxint. (There are many similar situations where a sentinel can be used to good effect. The resulting code is often easier to understand and never less efficient.)

See if you can understand how procedure InsertSort is used in the following more ambitious text processing application.

Example 7.2

```
program LetterSort (input, output);
(* This program reads a line of text terminated by *, saving any
   letters in vector letterlist. Output consists of letterlist
   sorted into natural order by a call of procedure InsertSort *)
const
   nmax = 100;   (* maximum number of letters *)
type
   range = 0..nmax;
   charvector = array[range] of char ;
var
   letterlist : charvector;
   i, n       : range;
   ch         : char;
procedure InsertSort (n : range;  var x : charvector);
(* Sorts the components 1,..,n of the char-valued vector x
   into non-decreasing order by insertion sort algorithm *)
   var
      i, j   : range;
      save   : char;
   begin
   x[0] := chr(0);    (* sentinel - the null character is less than
                         any other character *)
   for i := 2 to n do
      begin
      save := x[i];  j := i;
      while save < x[j-1] do
         begin
         x[j] := x[j-1];
         j := j-1
         end;
      x[j] := save
      end
   end (* InsertSort *);
function IsLetter (x : char) : boolean;
(* Returns true if the value of x is a letter of the alphabet,
   returns false otherwise *)
   begin
   IsLetter := (('a' <= x) and (x <= 'z')) or
               (('A' <= x) and (x <= 'Z'))
   end;
```

```
begin     (* main program *)
writeln;
writeln('I sort letters (zzzzzz.....)');
writeln; writeln('Enter a line of text terminated by *');

n := 0;   (* letter counter *)
repeat
   read(ch);
   if IsLetter(ch) then
      begin
      n := n+1;
      letterlist[n] := ch
      end
until ch = '*';

InsertSort(n, letterlist);

(* Output the sorted list *)
writeln;  writeln('Sorted list of letters is:');
for i := 1 to n do
   write(letterlist[i], ' ');
writeln
end.
```

Test runs:

```
I sort letters (zzzzzz.....)
```

Enter a line of text terminated by *
<u>+ - / *</u>

```
Sorted list of letters is:
```

[What's this?]

```
I sort letters (zzzzzz.....)
```

Enter a line of text terminated by *
<u>And everywhere that Mary went / Her Papa went 'Oh ****!'</u>

```
Sorted list of letters is:
A H M O P a a a a d e e e e e e h h h n n n p r r r r t t t t v w w
w y y
```

[Capital letters are 'less than' lower case in ASCII.]

8. Text Manipulation

Simple codes for text encryption are based on letter substitution: each letter is replaced by another letter or integer according to a fixed table (this is how characters are represented in the computer). Codes of this kind are easy to break, because common letters such as 'e' are encoded the same wherever they appear in the text.

More difficult for the cryptanalyst are codes where random numbers are used to determine the substitution. For example, with the 'random' number sequence

$$1 \quad 3 \quad 2 \quad 2 \quad 19 \quad 3 \quad 9 \quad 5$$

'A l l o 'a l l o
↓ ↓↓ ↓ ↓ ↓ ↓↓
'B o n q 't o u t

(what would the letter 'x' become if the corresponding number were, say, 3?)

In this chapter a program will be developed which reads a message typed at the keyboard and sends it to a file, either in enciphered form (called mode E) or in clear (mode C). A minor enhancement enables the program to read a message from a file and display the results on the screen, either deciphered (mode D) or in original form (mode F). This problem will introduce a number of important features of Pascal, in particular *text files* and *file parameters*.

8.1 Letter Substitution

Given a letter and an increment in the range 1..25, we encode the letter by shifting it cyclically the specified number of places in the alphabet:

     letter = 'A', increment = 1:   result 'B'
     letter = 'x', increment = 3:   result 'a'

The inverse of this (i.e. decoding) is effected by applying the negative of the increment to the coded letter, thus shifting it backwards the same number of places in the alphabet. These tasks are performed by

```
function subst (letter : char;  increment, base : integer) : char;
(* Encodes/decodes a single letter (the value of the char parameter
   letter) by adding a positive/negative increment to ord(letter),
   adjusting the result to be a letter of the same case.
   The value of base must be supplied as ord('a') for a lower-case
   letter or ord('A') for a capital letter *)
   var
      j : integer;
   begin
   j := ord(letter) + increment;
   (* Check that j represents a letter, adjust if necessary *)
   while j > base+25 do
      j := j-26;
   while j < base do
      j := j+26;
   subst := chr(j)
   end (* subst *);
```

Note that subst returns a char value; if we output it, the result will be B, a, etc.

For the increment parameter to subst we require a random integer. This is provided by a *pseudo-random number generator*, function rand below. For a given starting value, known as the *seed*, the parameter k assumes a sequence of values which are (statistically) random odd or even integers in the range $0..524287$. Of course the sequence is determined by the seed, hence 'pseudo'. One can do a lot of interesting things with random numbers. All we require is a random integer in the range $1..25$ or $-25..-1$, so we return $\pm(k \bmod 25 + 1)$.

```
function rand (var k : integer;  mode : char) : integer;
(* Returns a pseudo-random integer in the range 1..25 for encoding,
   -25..-1 for decoding *)
   begin
   k := (3125*k) mod 524288;
   if mode = 'E' then
      rand := k mod 25 + 1
   else
      rand := -(k mod 25 + 1)
   end (* rand *);
```

The mode parameter will have the value 'E' for encoding or 'D' for decoding (see program listing at the end of the chapter). Why is k a **var** parameter to this function?

8.2 Text Files

In addition to the standard files input and output, we may specify further file-names in the program heading, for example

```
program Crypto (input, output, codefile)
```

or

```
program Crunch (data1, data2, results)
```

The only files we shall consider are *text files*, which include those containing numeric data (text = **file of** char is a predefined data type). The text file codefile is *declared* in our program as

```
var
   codefile : text;
```

codefile may then be used as an additional data or results file. For this to be possible, when the program is executed the internal filename codefile has to be associated with a physical file on disk or other external storage medium. The arrangements for this are system dependent, and you should consult your local documentation or ask an instructor. (The familiar files input and output are predeclared text files associated with the keyboard and screen respectively; these default associations can similarly be overridden.)

To write to a user-declared text file, two statements are required in the program:

```
rewrite(codefile);   (* opens the file for output
                        clearing any previous contents *)
```

then at any later stage

```
write(codefile, x);
```

write(x) will still send output to the screen - in fact this is shorthand for write(output, x).

To read from a text file:

```
reset(codefile);   (* opens the file for input
                      starting at the beginning *)
```

then

```
read(codefile, x);
```

read(x) will still take input from the keyboard - this is shorthand for read(input, x).

We may thus have several channels of input and output in the same program.

8.3 Cipher and Crypto

Procedure `Cipher` is where most of the work is done. The basic operation is as follows: `Cipher` reads characters from an input stream called `infile` (more about this later). If the value of `mode` is `'E'` or `'D'`, the procedure checks whether each character is a letter and if so determines its case, then encodes/decodes it by calling `subst` and `rand` as previously explained. Any other character is left unchanged. Finally the character is written to an output stream called `outfile`.

Now we must consider some technical details. Lines of text (numeric as well as alphabetic data), whether read from the keyboard or a file, are marked by invisible *end-of-line markers*; if these are read as characters they are indistinguishable from the space character `' '`. When procedure `Cipher` reaches an end-of-line marker in `infile`, it must read past it and also start a new line in `outfile`. Pascal provides a boolean function `eoln` which returns `true` if and only if the reading position is at the end of a line, so we can achieve our purpose by a construct of the form

```
if eoln(infile) then
   begin
   readln(infile); writeln(outfile)
   end
```

(Incidentally, this is why `readln` rather than `read` is used for inputting numeric data under the control of **while not** `eof`; it is necessary to read past the final end-of-line marker to reach the end of file.)

`Infile` and `outfile` are *file parameters* to procedure `Cipher`; it is by these names that the procedure knows its input and output streams, and this is all it needs to know. Similarly, both `eoln` and `eof` can accept an optional file parameter which, if omitted, defaults to `input` (this is how we have used `eof` hitherto).

All these points are brought out in the following procedure.

```
procedure Cipher (var infile, outfile : text;  mode : char);
(* Enciphers ('E'), deciphers ('D') or copies ('C' or 'F') the
   text file infile, sending the results to outfile *)

   var
      ch : char;
      k  : integer;
      shiftletter : boolean;

   <function subst declared here as it is required only by Cipher>

   <function rand declared here for the same reason>
```

```
begin  (* body of Cipher *)
k := seed;    (* initial argument to pseudo-random number generator
               - seed is a program constant *)
shiftletter := (mode='D') or (mode='E');

while not eof(infile) do
    if eoln(infile) then
        begin
        readln(infile); writeln(outfile)
        end
    else
        begin
        read(infile, ch);
        if shiftletter then
            if ('a'<=ch) and (ch<='z') then    (* lower-case letter *)
                ch := subst(ch, rand(k,mode), ord('a'))
            else if ('A'<=ch) and (ch<='Z') then (* capital letter *)
                ch := subst(ch, rand(k,mode), ord('A'));
        write(outfile, ch)
        end
end  (* Cipher *);
```

The actual parameters to procedure Cipher, when it is called by the main program, occur in two combinations:

(1) (input, codefile, 'C' or 'E')
    - transmits characters from keyboard to file

(2) (codefile, output, 'D' or 'F')
    - transmits characters from file to screen.

You are recommended now to study the main program and see how the parts fit together.

Example 8.1

```
program Crypto (input, output, codefile);
(* This text processing program functions in four modes, selected by
the user:
E - enciphers a message typed at the keyboard, sending the results
    to codefile;
D - deciphers a message read from codefile, displaying the results
    on the screen;
C - copies a message in clear from the keyboard to codefile;
F - displays the contents of codefile on the screen.
Encryption is by letter substitution based on a pseudo-random
number sequence.
```

```
RESTRICTION: the enciphering/deciphering modes are designed to work
for a character representation such as ASCII in which letters of
the alphabet are coded as consecutive integers. The user should
verify that this is a valid assumption, for example by checking if
ord('Z')-ord('A') = 25 *)
const
    seed = 12345; (* to initialize the pseudo-random number generator,
                   may be set to any odd 5-digit integer *)

var
    mode     : char;
    codefile : text;

<procedure Cipher declared here with its
    subordinate functions subst and rand>

begin     (* main program *)
writeln;
writeln('Text encryption program using ''codefile'' ...');
        (* note that single quotes in a string must be doubled
            - the result appears as 'codefile' *)
writeln('Encipher, decipher, copy in clear or display file?');
repeat
    write('Enter E, D, C or F:  ');
    readln(mode)
until ('C' <= mode) and (mode <= 'F');
writeln;

if (mode = 'C') or (mode = 'E') then
    begin  (* copy or encipher message *)
    rewrite(codefile);
    writeln('Type your message, terminated by end-of-file marker:');
    writeln;
    Cipher(input, codefile, mode);
    writeln; writeln('Message sent to ''codefile''.')
    end
else
    begin  (* decipher or display file *)
    reset(codefile);
    writeln('Message in ''codefile'' reads:');
    writeln;
    Cipher(codefile, output, mode);
    writeln
    end
end.
```

Test runs:

```
Text encryption program using 'codefile' ...
Encipher, decipher, copy in clear or display file?
Enter E, D, C or F:  E
```

```
Type your message, terminated by end-of-file marker:
```

Mary had a little lamb,

Its fleece was sure to go.
```
^Z                      [or whatever the end-of-file marker is on your system]
```
```
Message sent to 'codefile'.
```


```
Text encryption program using 'codefile' ...
Encipher, decipher, copy in clear or display file?
Enter E, D, C or F:  F
```

```
Message in 'codefile' reads:
```

```
Ortx vif z tqamrp tcxw,
```

```
Uzx ifcqlc smt nwqs sq vi.
```


Another coded message:

```
   Efpffivttiabuya! Kq taa mdpc fjiaz ucg sfnwqfj ba fauxsytq vdor,
nbp rwzfmgf x kzarx-jygqg dfzwj ow mtja Qluapgjub bgszyuuzuvt.
   Idz hrxs vm hm nnp ehiu x jadcrgnyr jubx? Igh jbb ctaqu tq fcm cto
rqy oldte xd yssrg ydodvy qt jindh v dhvm zt cugf mzqe, tpjxf cx
peyoqlfz kco yfi zyuoux epk dwr yzjstg ljpnuy auynxjuag civ laa
vfopsvhp qb browb?
```

9. Recursion

9.1 Iteration and Recursion

The nth power of a given number x, where n is a positive integer, may be defined in two distinct ways:

$$x^n = x\, x \dots x \quad (n \text{ times}) \tag{9.1}$$

or

$$x^n = \begin{cases} x & \text{if } n = 1 \\ x\, x^{n-1} & \text{if } n > 1 \end{cases} \tag{9.2}$$

These definitions are completely equivalent as you can easily check, but they suggest two different methods of computing x^n.

The first method is *iterative*. From what we know of Pascal, we could implement (9.1) using a **for** statement (this has already been done in a more general form in example 5.2).

```
function PowerIter (x : real; n : integer) : real;
    var
        power : real;
        i     : integer;
    begin
    power := x;
    for i := 2 to n do
        power := power*x;
    PowerIter := power
    end;
```

The second method is more interesting. It is said to be *recursive*. At first sight (9.2) appears to be useless for actual computation, because it defines x^n in terms of x^{n-1} which is itself unknown unless $n = 2$. Nevertheless, we tentatively write the following function.

```
function PowerRecur (x : real; n : integer) : real;
   begin
   if n=1 then
      PowerRecur := x                              (* case A *)
   else
      PowerRecur := x*PowerRecur(x, n-1)           (* case B *)
   end;
```

In a construct of this form, A is called the *base* or *trivial case* and B the *recursive step*. Recursion implies that a function or procedure 'calls itself', possibly via other subprograms. Pascal, like all modern programming languages, allows this. The chain of recursive calls must eventually terminate in a trivial case such as A where some definite value can be calculated (or more generally some action executed). PowerRecur clearly satisfies this requirement; it is a valid function declaration in Pascal and will give the same results as PowerIter for n $\geq$ 1. (What happens if n $\leq$ 0?)

In fact, few programmers would use the recursive function here in preference to the iterative one. But there certainly are problems for which recursion is the most direct and appropriate means of formulating a solution.

Example 9.1
Consider again the nth power of x, now expressed in yet another way.

$$x^n = \begin{cases} x & \text{if } n = 1 \\ (x^{n/2})^2 & \text{if } n \text{ is even} \\ x\,(x^{(n-1)/2})^2 & \text{if } n \text{ is odd and } > 1 \end{cases} \qquad (9.3)$$

You should check that this is equivalent to the original definitions (9.1) and (9.2) (try various cases such as $n = 2, 3, 4$).

We can implement (9.3) as a recursive function to compute x^n.

```
function CleverPower (x : real; n : integer) : real;
   begin
   if n=1 then
      CleverPower := x
   else if odd(n) then
      CleverPower := x*sqr(CleverPower(x, n div 2))
   else
      CleverPower := sqr(CleverPower(x, n div 2))
   end;
```

For example, x^{20} is evaluated by CleverPower as

$$(x^{10})^2$$
$$= ((x^5)^2)^2$$
$$= ((x(x^2)^2)^2)^2$$

which, counting squaring as multiplication, requires only 5 multiplications. (The maximum *depth of recursion* is said to be 4 - to see this, follow down the chain of recursive calls and count them.) Clearly, for large n, this method requires far less arithmetic than the earlier methods.

Although it is possible to recast this in terms of iteration rather than recursion, it is by no means obvious how to go about it. You might see if you can devise an iterative version.

WARNING: Once a programmer has grasped the mechanics of recursion, she may be tempted to apply this technique indiscriminately to any process or formula that can be expressed in terms of recurrence relations. This is not always a clever thing to do.

Example 9.2

The Fibonacci numbers f_n, $n = 0,1,2,\ldots$, are defined by

$$f_0 = f_1 = 1$$
$$f_n = f_{n-1} + f_{n-2} \quad \text{for } n \geq 2$$

This definition might suggest a recursive Pascal function

```
function BadFib (n : integer) : integer;
   begin
   if n < 2 then
      BadFib := 1
   else
      BadFib := BadFib(n-1) + BadFib(n-2)
   end;
```

Although this function will correctly compute the Fibonacci number f_n, the efficiency of the computation leaves more than a little to be desired. The reason is that the values of $f_2, f_3, \ldots$ are worked out not just once (as they would be in an iterative version) but unnecessarily a large number of times. It is salutary to follow through the computation for $n = 6$: f_5 is computed once, f_4 twice, f_3 three times and f_2 five times. To compute the value of f_{30} by BadFib would require 2692537 recursive function calls!

9.2 The 'Towers of Hanoi'

This is a famous and venerable mathematical puzzle often used to demonstrate the real power of recursion. We have three pegs, A, B and C, and n discs all of different diameters, initially stacked in decreasing order on peg A.

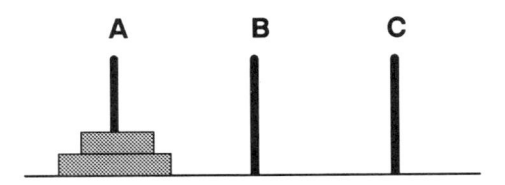

Figure 9.1 The Towers of Hanoi with n = 2 (almost trivial)

The problem is to move the n discs from A to B. *But*:
(1) only one disc may be moved at a time
(2) at every stage the discs on each peg must be stacked up in decreasing order of size
(3) no moves should be wasted.

The acolytes of an oriental temple have the task of solving this problem with 64 golden discs; when all the discs have been transferred from A to B in accordance with the rules, the universe will end. What is needed is a schedule of legal moves to accomplish the task. For $n = 2$ an optimal schedule is easily found. This is (see figure 9.1)

> move from A to C
> move from A to B
> move from C to B

where it is understood that the single topmost disc is to be moved every time (our monks are well versed in the rules).

For $n > 2$ the business gets more complicated, but as we shall see recursion can handle it.

Recursive Formulation

The essence of a recursive approach to a given problem (say of size n) is to reduce it to a set of *similar* problems of smaller sizes, and so on until trivial cases are reached, usually but not always corresponding to $n = 1$.

In this spirit let us suppose that we already know how to transfer $n-1$ discs between any two pegs according to the rules. Now consider the given problem of transferring n discs from A to B. If we first transfer the top $n-1$ discs from A to C (which we are assuming we know how to do!), then move the remaining (largest) disc from A to B, and finally transfer the $n-1$ discs back from C to B, we shall have solved the problem.

We denote by `Transfer (n, 'A', 'B' ,'C')` this hypothetical process of transferring *n* discs from A to B (with spare peg C). The solution sketched above can then be expressed more formally as

```
Transfer (n, 'A', 'B', 'C') :
   ⎧ Transfer (n-1, 'A', 'C', 'B')
   ⎨ Transfer (1, 'A', 'B', 'C)
   ⎩ Transfer (n-1, 'C', 'B', 'A')
```

This can be coded almost immediately as a recursive Pascal procedure (it is a procedure not a function since no values are computed; it is recursive because it 'calls itself' three times). However, we must use variables instead of constants for the peg names, because the role of the pegs changes continually as the recursion proceeds.

The trivial case ($n = 1$) amounts to moving a single disc, which is all that we really know how to do. Even though we do not know explicitly how to solve the problem for $n > 1$, we can supply the computer with a set of rules that it will obey until it produces the desired solution. It seems like magic - this is the power of recursion.

Example 9.3

```
program Hanoi (input, output);
(* This program solves the Towers of Hanoi problem for n discs.
   The value of n (1<=n<=nmax) is read in as data.
   If boolean constant trace is set to true, the schedule of moves
   is displayed, otherwise only the total number of moves is output *)
const
   nmax  = 64;    (* to keep the monks happy! *)
   trace = true;
type
   discs = 1..nmax;
   pegs  = 'A'..'C';   (* subrange of char *)
var
   n     : discs;
   count : integer;   (* global variable to count moves *)

procedure Transfer (n : discs;  origin, destination, spare : pegs);
(* Develops a schedule by recursion to transfer n discs from
   origin to destination *)
   begin
   if n=1 then
      begin     (* trivial case *)
      if trace then
         writeln('  move from ', origin, ' to ', destination);
      count := count+1
      end
```

```
    else
       begin       (* recursive steps *)
       Transfer(n-1, origin, spare, destination);
       Transfer(1, origin, destination, spare);
       Transfer(n-1, spare, destination, origin)
       end
    end (* Transfer *);
begin (* main program *)
writeln('Towers of Hanoi with n discs ...');
writeln;
write('Enter value of n (1<=n<=', nmax:2, '):  ');
readln(n);  writeln;
count := 0;
Transfer(n, 'A' ,'B', 'C');
writeln; writeln('Number of moves:', count:6)
end.
```

Test run:

```
Towers of Hanoi with n discs ...

Enter value of n (1<=n<=64):  3

   move from A to B
   move from A to C
   move from B to C
   move from A to B
   move from C to A
   move from C to B
   move from A to B

Number of moves:     7
```

[Follow this through to see how it solves the problem.]

Test run with trace set to false:

```
Towers of Hanoi with n discs ...

Enter value of n (1<=n<=64):  10

Number of moves:  1023
```

How many moves are required in general? Let u_n denote the number of moves required for n discs. From the recursive steps in procedure Transfer, we find that

$$u_n = 2u_{n-1} + 1 \quad \text{for } n > 1$$

and trivially $u_1 = 1$. It is straightforward to verify by substitution that this *difference equation* is satisfied by $u_n = 2^n - 1$, and in fact this is the only solution. Thus the time required depends exponentially on the problem size. For $n = 64$, assuming that each move takes one second, the task can be completed in 2^{64} seconds $\approx 10^{12}$ years.

10. Data Structures

What we have learnt so far of Pascal is more than adequate for understanding the numerical applications to be discussed in Parts 3 and 4 of this book. For the sake of completeness we now outline some other features of Pascal which, although only of marginal interest in the context of numerical computation, are of considerable importance in other computer science applications.

10.1 Record Types

As we have seen in chapter 4, an array is a structured data object whose individual components must all be of the same type. There are situations where it is useful to treat together a collection of entities which are not necessarily all of the same type. Pascal allows us to do this by means of the **record** facility.

Suppose that we wish to represent calendar dates, e.g. 31 Dec 1991. This consists of three identifiable components: the day (an integer in the range 1 to 31), the month (a three-character string), and the year (an integer). We can define our own Pascal type, date, and declare variables of this type as follows.

```
type
   date = record
            day   : 1..31;
            month : packed array[1..3] of char;
            year  : integer
          end;
var
   yesteryear : date;
```

Here day, month and year are called *field specifiers* and are used to reference the components or *fields* of the record. For example, we may assign values to the fields of yesteryear using the notation

```
yesteryear.day := 31;
yesteryear.month := 'Dec';
yesteryear.year := 1991
```

To express field references in a more succinct form, Pascal provides the **with** statement. The above assignments could be written alternatively as

```
with yesteryear do
    begin
    day := 31; month := 'Dec'; year := 1991
    end
```

If we combine records and arrays, we can set up quite sophisticated data structures (the use of pointers, to be introduced in section 10.3, adds a further level of flexibility). As a simple illustration, suppose that we wish to create a catalogue of famous people, recording name, profession, date of birth and birth-place. For example, the entry for Pascal (the man) would consist of

```
Surname:    Pascal
First name: Blaise
Profession: gentleman
Birthdate:  19 Jun 1623
Birthplace: Clermont-Ferrand
```

A suitable type definition might be

```
type
    string15 = packed array[1..15] of char;
    string20 = packed array[1..20] of char;
    celebrity = record
                    surname    : string20;
                    firstname  : string15;
                    profession : string15;
                    birthdate  : date;  (* itself a record *)
                    birthplace : string20
                end;
```

We could then declare a vector

```
catalogue : array[1..1000] of celebrity;
```

If Pascal's particulars above are stored as the 100th component, we could reference his surname as catalogue[100].surname, the initial letter of his first name as catalogue[100].firstname[1] (assuming there are no leading spaces), and his year of birth as catalogue[100].birthdate.year.

We illustrate the use of records with a mathematical application involving complex numbers.

Example 10.1

```
program ComplexPower (input, output);
(* This program computes the nth power of a complex number z
   by repeated multiplication; z and n>0 are read in as data *)
```

```
type
   complex = record
                re, im : real
             end;
var
   z, power : complex;
   j, n     : integer;

procedure cmult (u, v : complex; var product : complex);
(* Computes the complex product of u and v *)
   begin
   product.re := u.re * v.re - u.im * v.im;
   product.im := u.re * v.im + u.im * v.re
   end (* cmult *);

begin    (* main program *)
writeln; writeln('Complex number to the nth power ...');
writeln; write('Enter real and imaginary parts: ');
with z do
   readln(re, im);
repeat
   write('Enter positive integer n : ');  readln(n)
until n > 0;
writeln;

(* Compute power = z^n *)
power := z;
for j := 2 to n do
   cmult(z, power, power);

write('nth power = ');
with power do
   if im >= 0 then
      writeln(re:10:6, ' +',  im:10:6, 'i')
   else
      writeln(re:10:6, ' -', -im:10:6, 'i')
end.
```

Notes:
(1) The two fields of the record complex are of the same type, so we could have used an array complex[1..2] of real instead. The reason why a record type is preferred is readability: z.re and z.im are clearly more suggestive than z[1] and z[2].
(2) Since a Pascal function cannot return a composite value, cmult must be declared as a procedure.

Test run:

Complex number to the nth power ...

Enter real and imaginary parts: <u>2.341 -0.891</u>
Enter positive integer n : <u>4</u>

nth power =   4.559581 - 39.100154i

10.2 Set Types

Pascal is one of the very few programming languages which directly provide a data type for representing and manipulating mathematical sets, albeit only sets of elements chosen from some 'small' ordinal type. The maximum number of elements allowed in a Pascal set is implementation defined, but will normally be at least 32 and often 256.

The following **var** declaration introduces three set variables.

```
var
    charset  : set of char;
    smallint : set of 0..20;
    capitals : set of 'A'..'Z';
```

We may then assign values to these set variables by listing, in any order, the constituent elements or subranges of elements (of the specified type); for example,

```
charset  := ['0'..'9','+','-','.','e','E'];
smallint := [0,3];
capitals := ['A','E','H'..'J','M','R','S']
```

A set not containing any elements, the *empty set*, is denoted by [ ].

The following set-theoretic operations are provided:

operation	meaning	example of use	result
in	element relation	'Z' in capitals	false
+	set union	smallint + [1,3,12,9]	[0,1,3,9,12]
*	set intersection	charset * capitals	['E']
-	set difference	capitals - ['F'..'R']	['A','E','S']
= <>	set comparison	smallint = [1,5]	false
<=	subset relation	capitals <= charset	false
>=	superset relation	capitals >= ['A','E','I']	true

Operations are defined and meaningful only for sets having elements of compatible type; expressions such as smallint + charset or '0' in smallint are disallowed and should result in a compilation error.

Unless you are mathematically inclined, you will have little use for sets and set operations in your programs. There is, however, one situation where sets can be useful. Suppose we wish to test if a character variable ch represents a vowel. We could do this by a longwinded if statement of the form

```
if (ch='A') or (ch='a') ... or (ch='U') or (ch='u') then ...
```

Instead, we can make the vowels into a set and simply test

```
if ch in ['A','E','I','O','U','a','e','i','o','u'] then ...
```

which is much neater and also easier to understand.

10.3 Pointer Types

[The remainder of this chapter should be omitted on a first reading.]

A pointer value in Pascal is a *reference* to a program object of a kind to be described below; it may be thought of as representing the address of that object. With any Pascal type T, predefined or user-defined, there is associated a pointer type denoted by ↑T. For example,

```
type
   T = any type ;
var
   u : T;        (* variable of type T *)
   p : ↑T;       (* pointer variable of type ↑T *)
```

(Instead of ↑, which is not available on the keyboard, most implementations use the symbol ^ ; on some systems the symbol @ is used as an alternative.)

Initially, after declaration, a pointer variable p has an undefined value. To create an actual object of type T that p can point to, we use the predeclared procedure new. The invocation new(p) grabs one or more memory locations, suitable for holding values of type T, from a storage pool known as the *heap*, and assigns the start address (or equivalent) as the value of p. Values of type ↑T are of no direct concern and are therefore not normally accessible; an attempted output statement write(p) would be illegal.

The object pointed to by p is denoted by p↑. This symbol may appear on the left hand side of an assignment statement; this is how we assign a value to the object. Thus, p↑ serves as a 'name' for this anonymous object. In our example, let us suppose that T = integer; then, after invoking new(p),

```
p↑ := 100;  (* store 100 at the location referenced by p *)
write(2*p↑)
```

(output : 200)

The only operations apart from p↑ permitted on pointer variables are assignment, p := q (making p point to the same object as q), and equality testing, p = q or p <> q.

Example 10.2

```
program PointerTest (output);
(* This program illustrates the simple use of pointers.
   You should attempt to predict what output will be
   produced before you execute the program  *)

var
    x, y : ↑integer;

begin
new(x);  x↑ := 3;
new(y);   y↑ := 5;
writeln(x↑, y↑);
y↑ := 7;
x := y;          (* make x point to the same object as y *)
y↑ := 9;
writeln(x↑, y↑)
end.
```

An object created by new is said to be a *dynamic variable*. It continues to exist until program termination or until its memory allocation is returned to the heap by invocation of the predeclared procedure dispose (similarly, dynamic variables created during subprogram execution persist on exit). A dynamic variable persists even if all pointers originally referencing it have been re-assigned. Such an object cannot be referenced and is said to be *garbage*. For example,

```
new(x);  x↑ := 3;
new(y);  y↑ := 5;
y := x;           (* location containing 5 becomes garbage *)
dispose(x);       (* to avoid garbage, location containing 3 is
                     returned to heap before x is reassigned *)
new(x);  x↑ := 7
```

10.4 Linked Structures

What we have seen so far of pointers does not appear to be very useful. However, when data items and pointers are combined into a record structure to form a *cell*, it becomes possible to link together any number of these entities. This is a very powerful concept, as it allows us to represent dynamic data types such as stacks, queues and trees. Here, we shall only introduce the basic ideas.

Consider the following definitions.

```
type
    cellptr = ↑cell; (* the only situation where a data type,
                         i.e. cell, can be referred to before
                         it has been defined *)
    cell = record
               item : integer;  (* could be any data type *)
               next : cellptr
           end;
```

Suppose we declare two pointer variables,

```
var
    C, D : cellptr;
```

and create an object C↑ of type cell by invoking

```
new(C)
```

We may now assign an integer value to the item field of C↑ and nil to the next field,

```
C↑.item := 10;  C↑.next := nil
```

(nil is a special pointer value which indicates that the pointer does not reference any object). Doing the same with D,

```
new(D);
D↑.item := 5;  D↑.next := nil
```

we have the situation

If we now regard C as representing a list and wish to link in the additional cell D↑ at its head, we can make the following assignments:

```
D↑.next := C;  C := D
```

with the result

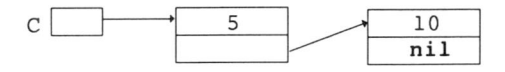

This process, which can be repeated as often as we wish, provides a basis for the construction of a *linear linked list*. All the data items stored in the various cells are accessible, that is, they may be changed or even deleted. We simply locate a cell by moving a pointer along the chain of links. Moreover, new cells can be linked anywhere into an existing list. Such a procedure is described in the following application.

Example 10.3
In section 7.3 we discussed the *insertion sort* algorithm. In this sorting method, data items are inserted at the correct position in a vector which is presumed to contain an already sorted sequence of elements. To make room for a new element, other elements have to be moved one place along the vector. Such a shifting process becomes unnecessary if instead of a vector we use a linked list to hold the data. If the list links together data items in non-decreasing order, we locate the cell after which a new element should be inserted, create a cell for it, and insert the cell into the list.

   We shall assume that the data items are strings comprising four characters - four-letter words for short. Given a string word, a cell for it is created by

```
function CreateCell (word : string;  link : cellptr) : cellptr;
(* This function makes a new cell initialized to word and link *)
    var
       c : cellptr;

    begin
    new(c);  (* create a new cell *)
    c↑.item := word;  c↑.next := link;
    CreateCell := c  (* function returns pointer to the cell *)
    end (* CreateCell *);
```

   The sorting process starts with an empty list which is trivially sorted. As in the original insertion sort method, it is convenient to make use of a 'sentinel'. In our application this must be the lexicographically last four-letter word, consisting of four tildes ˜˜˜˜ (ASCII code 126). What is needed is a procedure to find the correct position for each new cell to be inserted.

```
procedure Insert (word : string;  var chain : list);
(* This procedure inserts word at its correct place in chain.
   Note that chain is a pointer to the first cell in the list *)

    var
       p, q  : cellptr;

    begin
    if word <= chain↑.item then  (* word goes at start of chain *)
       chain := CreateCell(word, chain)
    else
       begin  (* find cell, pointed to by q, that precedes word *)
       p := chain;
       repeat
          q := p;
          p := p↑.next
       until word <= p↑.item;
```

```
          (* create new cell containing word and link it into chain *)
          q↑.next := CreateCell(word, p)
        end
    end (* Insert *);
```

We use these two subprograms in the following test program.

```
program MakeList (input, output);
(* This program reads a sequence of n-letter words and makes
   them into a lexicographically ordered linked list *)
const
   n = 4;                   (* length of word *)
   stopper = '~~~~';        (* n tildes - the last word *)
type
   string  = packed array[1..n] of char;
   cellptr = ↑cell;
   cell    = record
                 item : string;
                 next : cellptr
             end;
   list    = cellptr;  (* our linked list is represented by
                           a pointer to its first cell *)

var
    chain : list;
    p     : cellptr;
    word  : string;
    i     : 1..n;

<function CreateCell>

<procedure Insert>

begin     (* main program *)
writeln('Linked list demo (sorting ', n:1, '-letter words) ....');
writeln;
(* Create initial list consisting of sentinel cell *)
chain := CreateCell(stopper, nil);
repeat
   write('Enter a word or ', n:1, ' tildes to finish:  ');
   for i := 1 to n do
      read(word[i]);
   readln;
   if word <> stopper then
      Insert(word, chain);
until word = stopper;
```

```
writeln; writeln('Sorted list:'); writeln;
(* Output the words in the chain *)
p := chain;
while p↑.item <> stopper do
   begin
   write(p↑.item,' ');
   p := p↑.next
   end;
writeln
end.
```

Notes:

(1) To gain a better understanding of the pointer mechanism it is helpful to work through the program by hand, representing the various stages in diagrammatic form.

(2) The code can be simplified by the introduction of another sentinel element, '   ', which precedes any legitimate word. The initial list will then consist of two sentinel cells.

Test run:

```
Linked list demo (sorting 4-letter words) ....

Enter a word or 4 tildes to finish:  hunt
Enter a word or 4 tildes to finish:  hump
Enter a word or 4 tildes to finish:  dump
Enter a word or 4 tildes to finish:  duck
Enter a word or 4 tildes to finish:  open
Enter a word or 4 tildes to finish:  oven
Enter a word or 4 tildes to finish:  ~~~~

Sorted list:

duck dump hump hunt open oven
```

Exercise Set B

7.1 Write a program AllChange to read a line of text terminated by * and output it in reverse order with all lower-case letters converted to capitals and vice versa. Use the program to improve the first line of any recent pop song you know. Write another program to read a line of text and output it in correct order, but all words beginning with capital letters are to be output entirely in capitals and all others left unchanged.

7.2 Write a procedure to extract the initials of a person's name supplied to it as a string argument (with a terminating full stop). You may assume that at most one middle name is given, so the initials can be accommodated in a string of length three, with a space as the first character if no middle name is present. For example, Carl Friedrich Gauss becomes CFG, and Albert Einstein AE. Note that there may be several spaces before and between the names; your procedure should be able to cope with this eventuality.

7.3 Modify procedure InsertSort to sort a vector of strings of type string = **packed array**[1..len] **of** char, where len is specified as a program constant. Use this procedure in a program which inputs some text (a short verse, perhaps), and prints out the individual words in *lexicographic* order. Any punctuation marks should be ignored. You may assume that none of the words exceeds a length of fifteen - don't forget to pad any shorter words with trailing spaces.

8.1 A certain operating system provides the following facilities.

```
dog  file1  file2 ....
```

displays the contents of all the named files on the screen. The command

```
scribe
```

causes everything appearing on the screen, down to an end-of-file marker, to be saved in a file scribble. Unfortunately, dog has the effect of appending a control character to the end of every line, and so any 'dogged' programs saved in a scribble file are invalidated. Write a program to extract a text file contained in scribble, correct it and send the results to another file.

8.2 In an older style, Pascal programs were often written entirely in capitals. Write a program UglyPrint to read a Pascal program from a file and convert any lower-case letters to capitals, except those occurring in comments. A comment may be delimited by any combination of (*, { and *), }, with no nesting of brackets allowed. Send the results to another file. As a refinement, your program should be able to detect any syntactic errors in the comment structure and display a suitable error message on the screen.

8.3 Use the string sort procedure of exercise 7.3 (with len set to 3), and the procedure of exercise 7.2, in a program which inputs a list of names from a file, one name per line, extracts the initials and sorts the resulting list. Note that the ordering is determined first by the surname, i.e. the last initial (what comes next?). The sorted list of inititials should be sent to a results file.

9.1 Standard Pascal provides no power functions. Write a function Power(x,n) which can call CleverPower (from chapter 9) where appropriate, to compute x^n for any real x and integer n. Note that 0.0^n is undefined for $n \leq 0$. One possibility in this case would be to output an error message and force a runtime failure by attempting to compute $1/0$ (the compiler may try to prevent you from doing this but you can easily get around it). A spurious error message *attempted division by zero* will still be output - this is unavoidable.

9.2 Implement a representation of the stacks in program Hanoi (chapter 9). You could denote the discs by integers $1..n$ and use three vectors of type array[0..nmax] of integer, the zeroth component recording the number of discs on each stack. A 'move' then requires the program explicitly to move an element from one vector to another. Arrange to display the contents of the vectors after each move. Execute for $n = 5$ - it looks like a super-intelligence at work.

9.3 Write a recursive procedure to generate all the permutations of the integers $1..nmax$. (*Hint*: You may find it convenient to take the base of recursion as n = 0. There may be up to nmax recursive calls in the procedure; you can control these by a for loop.)

Extend your procedure to solve the *Eight Queens Problem*. This is the problem of arranging eight pieces on an 8×8 chessboard so that no two pieces lie on the same row, column or diagonal (the last constraint is the only one that requires modification of the program). How many different arrangements are there? Ignore the fact that the board has symmetries under which certain arrangements are equivalent.

10.1 Write a procedure `invert` to compute the reciprocal of a complex number (see example 10.1). Do not forget to check that the modulus is nonzero (what should be done if the modulus is zero?). Using this procedure, modify `program ComplexPower` to compute negative as well as positive powers of a complex number. How would you deal with a zero exponent?

10.2 Implement the idea of creating a catalogue of celebrities as suggested in section 10.1, using the given **record** type definition. You will have to write a suitable input routine to accept data from the keyboard or from a file. Data should be validated on input and suitable steps taken in case of errors - when done properly, data validation is not quite straightforward! Having successfully set up a catalogue, print a list of all physicists, mathematicians and gentlemen whose particulars have been recorded.

10.3 Write a test program to verify the results of the set-theoretic operations quoted in the table of section 10.2.

Determine the maximum number of elements allowed in a set on your Pascal system. Is it possible to declare set variables of type **set of** $1001..1003$? If not, why not?

10.4 Write a program which constructs a linked list of integer values read from a file or from the keyboard. The user will then specify two bounds `lo` and `hi`, whereupon your program should locate and delete all list cells whose values are within this specified range.

Part 3

Approximation

11. Least Squares Approximation

Example 11.1

Here is a set of measurements of the volume V of a quantity of gas kept at constant temperature as the pressure P is gradually increased.

P (bars)	1.000	1.200	1.300	1.500	1.600
V (litres)	0.755	0.621	0.577	0.498	0.474

From what we know of theory, we conjecture that V should be an approximately linear function of $1/P$. However, if V is plotted against $1/P$ it is found that the points do not lie exactly along a straight line. The discrepancies are presumed to be due to random experimental errors in the measurement of volume.

What is the equation of a line that would best represent the behaviour of the gas in this experiment, and how closely can the line be made to fit the data? In this chapter we will develop tools to answer these and related questions.

11.1 The Principle of Least Squares

Given a set of m points in the xy-plane, $(x_1, f_1), ..., (x_m, f_m)$ where m may be large, we have the problem of finding a simple curve $y = p(x)$ that best fits the data. The form of the function $p(x)$ - linear, quadratic, exponential etc - is usually suggested by theoretical considerations in the application area. Such a curve is not expected to pass through all or perhaps any of the data points: the *deviations* $R_i = p(x_i) - f_i$, $i = 1, ..., m$, may be positive or negative but will in general be nonzero (see figure 11.1).

There are various possible criteria for 'best fit'. A reasonable requirement would be to make the sum of the R_i equal to zero, but this is not sufficient in itself to fix the curve. In the *least squares method* we consider the *sum of squares* of the deviations,

$$
\begin{aligned}
S &= \sum_{i=1}^{m} R_i^2 \\
&= \sum_{i=1}^{m} (p(x_i) - f_i)^2 \geq 0
\end{aligned}
$$

and choose the parameters of p in order to minimize S.

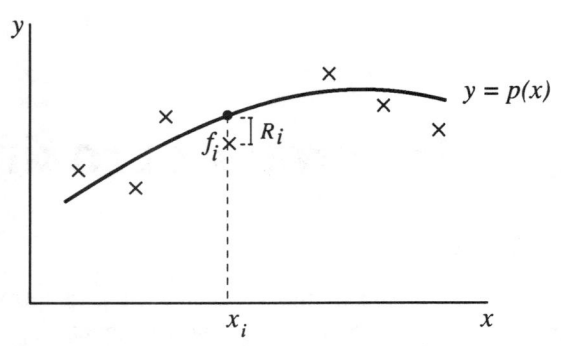

Figure 11.1   The deviation $R_i = p(x_i) - f_i$

Straight Line Fitting

The simplest case is a straight line law, $p(x) = a + bx$. Then
$$S = \Sigma (a + bx_i - f_i)^2$$
(summation from 1 to m will be understood). Although a and b are constant coefficients of a certain straight line, they are at this stage unknown, and $S = S(a, b)$ is a function of these two unknowns. The least squares problem is to determine a and b, and hence p, so as to minimize S.

The function S can be minimized with respect to a and b by the usual methods of calculus, setting $\partial S/\partial a$ and $\partial S/\partial b$ to zero (these conditions are necessary and in the present case sufficient for a minimum). We find
$$\partial S/\partial a = 2\Sigma (a + bx_i - f_i)$$
$$\partial S/\partial b = 2\Sigma (a + bx_i - f_i)\, x_i$$
giving, with $\Sigma a = ma$, the so-called *normal equations*
$$a\,m \;+\; b\Sigma x_i \;=\; \Sigma f_i$$
$$a\Sigma x_i \;+\; b\Sigma x_i^2 \;=\; \Sigma x_i f_i \tag{11.1}$$
This is a pair of simultaneous linear equations easily solvable for the unknowns a and b. The resulting straight line $y = a + bx$ gives a smoothed representation of the data on the assumption of random errors in the f_i values.

Having found a and b, we can calculate the deviations $R_i = a + bx_i - f_i$ for $i = 1, ..., m$, then the sum $S = \Sigma R_i^2$, and finally the *root mean square deviation* $(S/m)^{1/2}$. This will be a measure of how closely the straight line fits the data.

Application to Example 11.1

$x = 1/P$	$f = V$	x^2	xf	$a + bx$	R
1.0000	0.755	1.0000	0.7550	0.752	−0.003
0.8333	0.621	0.6944	0.5175	0.626	0.005
0.7692	0.577	0.5917	0.4438	0.578	0.001
0.6667	0.498	0.4445	0.3320	0.501	0.003
0.6250	0.474	0.3906	0.2963	0.469	−0.005
$\Sigma =$ 3.8942	2.925	3.1212	2.3446		0.001

The normal equations (11.1) are, with $m = 5$,

$$5a + 3.8942b = 2.925$$
$$3.8942a + 3.1212b = 2.3446$$

from which, working to 4 decimal places and rounding to 3, we find

$$a = -0.002, \quad b = 0.754$$

Thus $V = -0.002 + 0.754/P$ is the best (least squares straight line) fit.

With these results for a and b, we can now find the values of $a + bx$ corresponding to the data points and calculate the deviations $R = a + bx - f$ ($\Sigma R = 0$ theoretically: note the effect of rounding error in the third decimal place). The root mean square deviation $(\Sigma R^2/m)^{\frac{1}{2}}$ is found to be $(69/5)^{\frac{1}{2}} \times 10^{-3}$ = 0.004. This is a measure of the typical deviation of the straight line from the data. With a larger data set we could also examine the distribution of + and − signs in the R column; a systematic clustering would indicate that some non-linear curve might give a better representation.

In realistic cases there are usually far more data than in example 11.1, and it is highly desirable to develop a program so the work can be done by computer. The following is a straightforward implementation of the method used above.

Example 11.2

```
program LineFit (input, output);
(* This program fits a straight line y = a + bx to a set of data
   points (x[i],f[i]), i=1,...,m (m <= datamax) by least squares
   approximation.
   Input: a sequence of real number pairs x f, one pair on each line.
   Output: the coefficients a and b, followed by the root mean square
   deviation *)
```

```pascal
const
   datamax = 100;   (* maximum permitted number of data points *)

var
   i, m   : integer;
   x, f   : array[1..datamax] of real;
   sumx, sumf, sumxf, sumxsq, sumrsq, mult, a, b : real;

begin
(* Input the data *)
m := 0;
while not eof and (m < datamax) do
   begin
   m := m+1;
   readln(x[m], f[m])
   end;

writeln('Least squares straight line fit, y = a + bx ...');
writeln;
if not eof then   (* too many data points *)
   writeln('WARNING: Only ', datamax:3, ' data points allowed');
writeln('Number of data points used: ', m:3);   writeln;

if m < 2 then
   writeln('ERROR: Insufficient data')
else
   begin
   (* Accumulate the sums *)
   sumx := 0; sumf := 0; sumxsq := 0; sumxf := 0;
   for i := 1 to m do
      begin
      sumx := sumx + x[i];   sumf := sumf + f[i];
      sumxsq := sumxsq + sqr(x[i]);   sumxf := sumxf + x[i]*f[i]
      end;
   (* Solve the normal equations *)
   mult := sumx/sumxsq;
   a := (sumf-mult*sumxf) / (m-mult*sumx);
   b := (sumxf-a*sumx) / sumxsq;
   writeln('   a = ', a:10);   writeln('   b = ', b:10);
   writeln;
   (* Calculate RMS deviation *)
   sumrsq := 0;
   for i := 1 to m do
      sumrsq := sumrsq + sqr(a+b*x[i]-f[i]);
   writeln('RMS deviation = ', sqrt(sumrsq/m):10)
   end
end.
```

Test run:

As a first check we run the program on the data $(1/P, V)$ of example 11.1.

```
Least squares straight line fit, y = a + bx ...

Number of data points used:   5

    a = -1.847e-03
    b =  7.535e-01

RMS deviation =  3.677e-03
```

11.2 Exponential Curves

In many problems of science and engineering, the data, which we now denote by (x_i, g_i), $i = 1, ..., m$, will follow an exponential law of the form $y = A\,e^{bx}$. The least squares method would then require us to minimize $S = \Sigma\,(A\,e^{bx_i} - g_i)^2$ with respect to A and b. Setting $\partial S/\partial A$ and $\partial S/\partial b$ to zero gives a pair of nonlinear equations which could be solved by approximation methods, but not easily.

Instead, it is common practice to *linearize* the problem by taking logarithms and fitting $y = \log_e A + bx$ to $(x_i, \log_e g_i)$, $i = 1, ..., m$. With $a = \log_e A$ and $f_i = \log_e g_i$, this is the straight line case which we already know how to solve. (It is actually a different approximation problem from the original nonlinear one, but as the least squares criterion is itself somewhat arbitrary this is usually ignored.)

Example 11.3

The following measurements of a quantity $g(t)$, believed on theoretical grounds to be a decreasing exponential function of t, were recorded in an experiment.

t	1	2	3	4	5
$g(t)$	0.905	?	0.337	0.201	0.123

Unfortunately, the reading for $t = 2$ was lost when J. Bloggs pulled the plug. Find the best curve to fit the data by the linearized least squares method and hence estimate $g(2)$.

We execute `program LineFit` on the logarithmized data

1	−0.0998
3	−1.0877
4	−1.6045
5	−2.0956

with the results

```
Least squares straight line fit, y = a + bx ...

Number of data points used:    4

    a =    4.028e-01
    b = -4.999e-01

RMS deviation =   6.173e-03
```

Since $A = e^a = 1.496$, the curve is $y = 1.496\ e^{-0.500t}$, and the missing value $g(2) \approx y(2) = 0.550$.

11.3 Polynomial Fitting

In some applications a quadratic or higher-degree polynomial might be the appropriate choice. We can apply the least squares method to a polynomial of degree n, $p_n(x) = a_0 + a_1 x + \ldots + a_n x^n$, by considering

$$S = \Sigma (a_0 + a_1 x_i + \ldots + a_n x_i^n - f_i)^2$$

The function S can be minimized with respect to $a_0, a_1, \ldots, a_n$ in the usual way, giving $n + 1$ *linear equations* for the $n + 1$ desired coefficients.

We demonstrate this for $n = 2$. For the quadratic $a_0 + a_1 x + a_2 x^2$ we have

$$S = \Sigma (a_0 + a_1 x_i + a_2 x_i^2 - f_i)^2$$

then

$$\partial S / \partial a_0 = 2 \Sigma (a_0 + a_1 x_i + a_2 x_i^2 - f_i)$$
$$\partial S / \partial a_1 = 2 \Sigma (a_0 + a_1 x_i + a_2 x_i^2 - f_i)\, x_i$$
$$\partial S / \partial a_2 = 2 \Sigma (a_0 + a_1 x_i + a_2 x_i^2 - f_i)\, x_i^2$$

The three normal equations are

$$\begin{aligned}
a_0\, m &+ a_1 \Sigma x_i &+ a_2 \Sigma x_i^2 &= \Sigma f_i \\
a_0 \Sigma x_i &+ a_1 \Sigma x_i^2 &+ a_2 \Sigma x_i^3 &= \Sigma x_i f_i \\
a_0 \Sigma x_i^2 &+ a_1 \Sigma x_i^3 &+ a_2 \Sigma x_i^4 &= \Sigma x_i^2 f_i
\end{aligned}$$

Once the required sums have been computed from the data, these equations can be solved for a_0, a_1, a_2 without difficulty.

We now give a procedure to set up the $n + 1$ normal equations for a polynomial of degree n. It should be clear that the only sums that need to be computed directly are those appearing in the top row, the right hand column and the right hand side of the equations; the rest can be filled in by copying once these segments are complete. This is what our procedure does. Follow it through step by step for the case $n = 2$ to see how it works. The following constants and data types are used:

```
datamax    (* maximum permitted number of data points *)
nmax       (* maximum degree of approximating polynomial *)
nmaxplusl

degree   = 0..nmax;
datavec  = array[1..datamax] of real;
coeffmat = array[degree, 0..nmaxplusl] of real;
```

Example 11.4

```
procedure SetUp (m : integer;  n : degree;  var x, f : datavec;
                 var C : coeffmat);
(* Sets up normal equations for polynomial approximation of degree n
   to data (x[i],f[i]), i=1,...,m, where n < m <= datamax.
   The coefficients of the n+1 normal equations are returned in
   columns 0..n of array C, the right hand side in column n+1 *)

var
    i : integer;
    k : degree;
    power : real;

begin
(* Initialization of row 0, column n and column n+1 *)
C[0,0] := m;
for k := 1 to n do
    begin
    C[0,k] := 0;
    C[k,n] := 0; C[k,n+1] := 0
    end;
C[0,n+1] := 0;

(* Accumulate sums in array C *)
for i := 1 to m do
    begin
    C[0,n+1] := C[0,n+1] + f[i];
    power := 1;
    for k := 1 to n do
        begin
        power := power*x[i];
        C[0,k] := C[0,k] + power;
        C[k,n+1] := C[k,n+1] + power*f[i]
        end;
```

```
for k := 1 to n do
   begin
   power := power*x[i];
   C[k,n] := C[k,n] + power
   end
end;
(* Complete array C by copying *)
for k := 1 to n do
   begin
   for i := 1 to k do
      C[i,k-i] := C[0,k];
   for i := k+1 to n do
      C[i,n+k-i] := C[k,n]
   end
end (* SetUp *);
```

We still have the problem of solving $n + 1$ linear equations to determine the parameters a_0, a_1, ..., a_n of the least-squares polynomial $p_n(x)$. This is deferred until we have discussed systems of linear equations in chapter 17.

Further Developments

What we have been considering in this chapter is *discrete* least squares approximation: given a function $f(x)$, 'numerically defined' by its values on a finite set $\{x_1, x_2, ..., x_m\}$, we approximate it by a function $p(x)$ which may be polynomial, exponential etc. We have assumed that the values $f(x_i)$ contain random experimental errors and it would be inappropriate to require the function $p(x)$ to agree precisely with the given data. On the other hand, if the data were essentially exact, such as entries in a mathematical table or points on a contour in computer graphics, it would be reasonable to construct a curve which passed exactly through all the data points. This approach is taken up in chapter 12.

The least squares method can be extended to approximate a function $f(x)$ defined in the more familiar way by a formula. We seek to represent $f(x)$ by a simpler function $p(x)$ over some interval $a \leq x \leq b$. Instead of the sum of squares of the deviations, we have to minimize

$$S = \int_a^b (p(x) - f(x))^2 dx$$

by a suitable choice of the parameters of p. The details can be found in more comprehensive textbooks of numerical analysis; the basic ideas are not difficult but would take us too far out of our course.

12. Interpolation

Example 12.1
A mathematician is shipwrecked on a desert island. After building a raft, he decides it would be a good idea to compile a table of trigonometric values: $\sin x$, $x = 0° (10°) 90°$. This might come in useful for navigation; anyway it will pass the time until the trade winds start.

He has no mathematical tables and his calculator went down with the ship. How can he do it? Can he, for example, calculate $\sin 50°$? If so, how much confidence can he place in the answer?

12.1 Linear and Quadratic Interpolation

Two points in the xy-plane, (x_0, f_0) and (x_1, f_1) with $x_0 \neq x_1$, determine a straight line $y = p_1(x)$ that passes through both points:

$$p_1(x) = \frac{x - x_1}{x_0 - x_1} f_0 + \frac{x - x_0}{x_1 - x_0} f_1$$

(check by evaluating $p_1(x)$ at $x = x_0$ and $x = x_1$).

Given three points (x_0, f_0), (x_1, f_1) and (x_2, f_2), we can do better. There is a quadratic curve that passes through all three points, again provided that none of x_0, x_1, x_2 coincide. The quadratic can be expressed as

$$p_2(x) = \frac{(x - x_1)(x - x_2)}{(x_0 - x_1)(x_0 - x_2)} f_0 + \frac{(x - x_0)(x - x_2)}{(x_1 - x_0)(x_1 - x_2)} f_1 + \frac{(x - x_0)(x - x_1)}{(x_2 - x_0)(x_2 - x_1)} f_2 \qquad (12.1)$$

(check that $p_2(x_0) = f_0$, $p_2(x_1) = f_1$, $p_2(x_2) = f_2$ as required).

It is easy to show that $p_2(x)$, or a function equivalent to it, is the only quadratic with this property. To see this, suppose there is another quadratic $q(x)$ that passes through the same three points, and consider the function

$$r(x) = p_2(x) - q(x)$$

At $x = x_0$, $r(x_0) = p_2(x_0) - q(x_0) = f_0 - f_0 = 0$. Similarly $r(x_1) = f_1 - f_1 = 0$ and $r(x_2) = f_2 - f_2 = 0$. Now since $r(x)$ itself is at most quadratic, we would have a quadratic equation $r(x) = 0$ with three distinct roots, $x = x_0, x_1, x_2$, which is impossible unless $r(x)$ is identically zero (i.e. zero everywhere). But this is the same as saying that $q(x) \equiv p_2(x)$.

Application to Example 12.1

The castaway remembers the following values of sin x (x in degrees).

x	0	30	90
sin x	0	0.5	1.0

He wants an approximation to sin x at, say, $x = 50$. He can use *quadratic interpolation*, substituting the values from the table into equation (12.1) above.

$$\sin 50° \approx p_2(50)$$

$$= 0 + \frac{(50-0)(50-90)}{(30-0)(30-90)} \times 0.5 + \frac{(50-0)(50-30)}{(90-0)(90-30)} \times 1.0$$

$$= 0.7407$$

12.2 Lagrange's Formula

The general case: given $n + 1$ data points (x_0, f_0), ..., (x_n, f_n), where none of the nodes $x_0, ..., x_n$ coincide, there is a unique *interpolating polynomial* of degree $\leq n$ which can be expressed as

$$p_n(x) = L_0(x)f_0 + ... + L_i(x)f_i + ... + L_n(x)f_n$$

where

$$L_i(x) = \frac{(x-x_0) \, ... \, (x-x_{i-1})(x-x_{i+1}) \, ... \, (x-x_n)}{(x_i-x_0) \, ... \, (x_i-x_{i-1})(x_i-x_{i+1}) \, ... \, (x_i-x_n)} \tag{12.2}$$

for $i = 0, 1, ..., n$. This is *Lagrange's formula*. As in the cases $n = 1, 2$ above, you are recommended to check that $p_n(x_i) = f_i$ for $0 \leq i \leq n$. In a similar way to the case $n = 2$ it can be proved that the interpolating polynomial $p_n(x)$ is unique, meaning that there is no other distinct polynomial of degree $\leq n$ that passes through all the points (x_0, f_0), ..., (x_n, f_n).

Our intention is to use the polynomial $p_n(x)$ to approximate a function $f(x)$ at some arbitrary point $x = \bar{x}$. Lagrange's formula for this is easy to program, although as we shall see later in this chapter there is a better, more flexible method (Neville's algorithm) for arriving at the same result.

Example 12.2

```
program Interpolate (input, output);
(* This program approximates the value of f(x) at x=xbar by polynomial
   interpolation on the data (x[i],f[i]), i=0,...,n, where n<=maxdeg.
   Input: the required point xbar, followed by a sequence of real
   number pairs  x   f, one pair on each line.
   Output: the value xbar and the number of data points, followed by
   an approximation to f(xbar).
   No bound or error estimate is provided by this program *)

const
    maxdeg = 10; (* maximum degree of interpolating polynomial *)

type
    degree  = 0..maxdeg;
    datavec = array[degree] of real;

var
    x, f  : datavec;
    xbar  : real;
    n     : integer;

function Lagrange (n : degree;  var x, f : datavec;
                                xbar : real) : real;
(* Computes an approximation to f(xbar) by Lagrangian interpolation
   of degree n on the data points (x[i],f[i]), i=0,...,n *)

    var
        sum, L : real;
        i, j   : degree;

    begin
    sum := 0;
    for i := 0 to n do
        begin
        L := 1;
        for j := 0 to n do
            if j<>i then
                L := L*(xbar-x[j])/(x[i]-x[j]);
                (* see Lagrange's formula *)
        sum := sum + L*f[i]
        end;
    Lagrange := sum
    end (* Lagrange *);
```

```
begin (* main program *)
readln(xbar);
n := -1;
while not eof and (n < maxdeg) do
   begin
   n := n+1;
   readln(x[n], f[n])
   end;

writeln;
writeln('Polynomial interpolation of degree <=', maxdeg:3, ' ...');
writeln;
writeln('Point at which approximation required:   x =', xbar:6:2);
writeln;
if not eof then   (* too many data points *)
   writeln('WARNING: Only ', (maxdeg+1):2, ' data points allowed');

writeln('Number of data points used:', (n+1):3);   writeln;
writeln('Estimate of f(x) =', Lagrange(n, x, f, xbar) :8:4);
writeln('based on interpolating polynomial of degree', n:3);
writeln
end.
```

Test run:

We execute the program on the following data to approximate sin 50°.

```
   50
    0    0.0
   30    0.5
   90    1.0
  150    0.5
  180    0.0
```

```
Polynomial interpolation of degree <= 10 ...

Point at which approximation required:   x = 50.00

Number of data points used:  5

Estimate of f(x) =   0.7668
based on interpolating polynomial of degree   4
```

What can be said about the accuracy of this result? To answer this question, we need to examine in more detail the error of polynomial interpolation, $E = f(\overline{x}) - p_n(\overline{x})$.

Theorem 12.1 (Error of Interpolation)
Let $[a, b]$ be an interval containing all the nodes $x_0, ..., x_n$. If $f(x)$ has an $(n + 1)$st derivative, denoted by $f^{(n+1)}(x)$, everywhere in this interval, then the error of the interpolating polynomial $p_n(x)$ at any point $x = \bar{x}$ in $[a, b]$ is given by

$$E = \frac{(\bar{x} - x_0) \cdots (\bar{x} - x_n)}{(n + 1)!} f^{(n+1)}(\xi)$$

where ξ is an unknown point dependent on $\bar{x}$, satisfying $a < \xi < b$.

A proof of this theorem can be found in standard textbooks of numerical analysis. In our case we know that $f(x) = \sin x$, $n = 4$ and $\bar{x} = 5\pi/18$ (as we are going to employ differentiation we must remember to use radians). Thus $f^{(n+1)}(\xi) = \cos \xi$, since $d^5(\sin x)/dx^5 = \cos x$. According to Theorem 12.1 the error is

$$E = \bar{x}(\bar{x} - \pi/6)(\bar{x} - \pi/2)(\bar{x} - 5\pi/6)(\bar{x} - \pi)(\cos \xi)/5!$$
$$= -0.0070 \cos \xi$$

Again according to the theorem, $0 < \xi < \pi$, so $|\cos \xi| < 1$, and we can state an *error bound*: $|E| < 0.0070$. We conclude that $\sin 50° = 0.7668 \pm 0.0070$ [true value: $\sin 50° = 0.7660...$].

12.3 Neville's Algorithm

The error formula for polynomial interpolation (Theorem 12.1) is difficult to work with; it may be impossible to use in practice even if an expression is known for $f(x)$. What is sometimes done instead is to compute a sequence of approximations to $f(\bar{x})$ based on polynomials of increasing degree, adding more data points until agreement is obtained to the required accuracy. The drawback of using Lagrange's formula for this purpose is that each L_i function (12.2) involves all the nodes $x_0, ..., x_n$, and so the entire formula has to be recalculated if any further data points are added.

A more flexible approach is *Neville's algorithm*. This is still based on evaluating the interpolating polynomial and so gives the same results, but the method is organized in a more efficient way. Let $p_{i,j}(x)$ denote the interpolating polynomial which agrees with $f(x)$ at each of $x_i, x_{i+1}, ..., x_j$. For example, $p_{0,1}(x)$ is the straight line passing through the two points (x_0, f_0), (x_1, f_1). Now consider the expression

$$\frac{(x - x_j) p_{i,j-1}(x) - (x - x_i) p_{i+1,j}(x)}{x_i - x_j} \tag{12.3}$$

At $x = x_i$ this reduces to $p_{i,j-1}(x_i) = f_i$, since $p_{i,j-1}$ agrees with f at x_i. Similarly at $x = x_j$ the value is $p_{i+1,j}(x_j) = f_j$, for a similar reason. At each node x_k where $i < k < j$, both $p_{i,j-1}(x)$ and $p_{i+1,j}(x)$ have the value f_k, and it is easily verified that the value of (12.3) is f_k. Thus the above expression agrees with $f(x)$ at $x = x_i, x_{i+1},...,x_j$; it is the interpolating polynomial $p_{i,j}(x)$ by definition.

Neville's algorithm consists in building up the interpolating polynomials (linear, quadratic, cubic etc) by formula (12.3), in practice evaluated at a particular point $x = \bar{x}$. The results can be set out in a triangular table

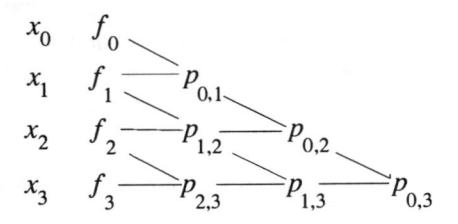

For example, the case $i = 0, j = 3$ of (12.3) gives

$$p_{0,3}(\bar{x}) = \frac{(\bar{x} - x_3)p_{0,2}(\bar{x}) - (\bar{x} - x_0)p_{1,3}(\bar{x})}{x_0 - x_3}$$

as indicated by the rightmost lines in the diagram. The value $p_{0,3}(\bar{x})$ is the approximation to $f(\bar{x})$ obtained from the interpolating cubic on the data points $(x_0, f_0), ..., (x_3, f_3)$.

The attraction of this method is that the above table can be computed row by row. If further data points are added, it is a simple matter to extend the table by constructing extra rows. For an 'estimated error bound' we follow the common practice of comparing the values $p_{1,j}(\bar{x})$ and $p_{0,j-1}(\bar{x})$, obtained from the two interpolating polynomials of degree $j-1$, with $p_{0,j}(\bar{x})$, and take the larger of the two differences. It should be emphasized that in general this does *not* give a guaranteed error bound; for that our only recourse would be to Theorem 12.1.

Our procedure for Neville's algorithm follows this description fairly closely. The main refinement is that, for the reasons explained, a 2-dimensional array is not required; computing row by row, all we need is an old row vector p and a new row vector q. The vectors p, q, x and f are of type

```
        datavec = array[degree] of real;
where
        degree  = 0..maxdeg;
```

Example 12.3

```
procedure Neville (n : degree;  var x, f : datavec; xbar, tol : real;
                   var fxbar, errbnd : real;  var m : degree);
(* This procedure computes an approximation fxbar to the value of
   f(x) at x=xbar by polynomial interpolation on the data (x[i],f[i]),
   i=0,...,n, using Neville's algorithm.
   The computation terminates in one of two ways:
   (1) all n+1 data points have been used, or
   (2) an estimated error bound for fxbar is found to be less than
       the user-supplied tolerance tol after m+1 points (x[i],f[i]),
       i=0,...,m, have been used, with m < n.
   In either case an estimated error bound is returned in errbnd
   with a default value of 1.0e10 in the case n=0 *)

   var
       p, q       : datavec;   (* old and new rows of Neville table *)
       i, j, k    : degree;
       est1, est2 : real;      (* estimates of error bound *)

   begin
   q[0] := f[0];
   j := 0;   errbnd := 1.0e10;  (* default error bound *)
   while (j < n) and (errbnd > tol) do
      begin
      for k := 0 to j do
         p[k] := q[k]; (* save old row *)
      j := j+1;
      q[0] := f[j];       (* start new row *)
      for k := 1 to j do
         begin
         i := j-k;
         q[k] := ((xbar-x[j])*p[k-1]-(xbar-x[i])*q[k-1])
                 /(x[i]-x[j])
                 (* see Neville's formula *)
         end;
      est1 := abs(q[j]-q[j-1]);  est2 := abs(q[j]-p[j-1]);
      if est1 > est2 then
         errbnd := est1
      else
         errbnd := est2
      end;
   fxbar := q[j];  m := j
   end (* Neville *);
```

Further Developments

Attempting to approximate a function by a single interpolating polynomial of high degree (say 6 or more), especially with equally-spaced data, can give rise to severe difficulties. It is not guaranteed that interpolating polynomials based on an increasing number of equally-spaced nodes in a given interval will converge uniformly to the function; large fluctuations may appear near the ends of the interval. An alternative approach much favoured in practice is *piecewise interpolation*: in each subinterval between successive data points a different 'simple' curve is fitted, with some conditions at the joins to ensure smoothness.

In the popular *cubic spline* method the piecewise curves are chosen to be cubic polynomials. An interpolating cubic has two degrees of freedom remaining after the end points have been fixed, leaving enough flexibility to provide for continuity in the first and second derivatives at the joins. The resulting composite curve is very smooth, but with the disadvantage that a system of linear equations has to be solved to construct it. If less smoothness is tolerable, as is often the case in computer graphics, a range of methods has been developed to fit piecewise curves at lower computational cost while still producing visually acceptable results.

13. Numerical Integration

Example 13.1

The molecules of an ideal gas have speeds distributed between 0 and ∞, with a peak or most probable speed $\hat{v}$ determined by the temperature. According to Maxwell's distribution law, the proportion of molecules with speeds up to $\alpha\hat{v}$ for any $\alpha \geq 0$ is given by

$$p(\alpha) = \frac{4}{\sqrt{\pi}} \int_0^\alpha x^2 e^{-x^2} dx$$

For example, $p(2)$ is a certain number which is expected on physical grounds to lie between 0 and 1; but there is no way of calculating it analytically (no transformation or substitution can be found to evaluate the integral).

Many such intractable integrals arise in scientific and engineering practice, and these must be evaluated by approximation methods. In this chapter we will develop a program with the aim of computing definite integrals automatically to a prescribed accuracy.

13.1 The Trapezoidal Rule

One of the simplest ways to approximate an integral $I = \int_a^b f(x)dx$ is to replace the curve $y = f(x)$ by an interpolating straight line, taking the area of the resulting trapezium (see figure 13.1) as an approximation to I.

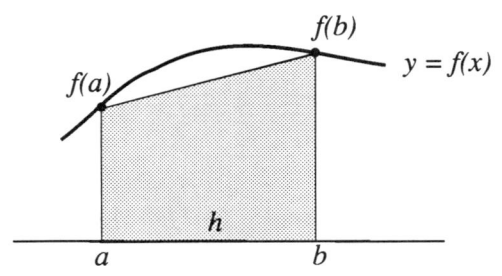

Figure 13.1 The basic trapezoidal rule

111

Writing $h = b - a$, we have

$$I \approx h(f(a) + f(b))/2$$

This is the *basic trapezoidal rule*.

It seems plausible that the accuracy of the approximation can be improved if we divide the range of integration $[a, b]$ into n subintervals of *step size* $h = (b - a)/n$ and apply the basic rule repeatedly, adding up n contributions. Writing $f_i = f(a + ih)$, $i = 0,1,\ldots,n$, we obtain the *composite trapezoidal rule*

$$\begin{aligned} I &\approx T_h \\ &= h(f_0/2 + f_1 + \ldots + f_{n-1} + f_n/2) \end{aligned} \tag{13.1}$$

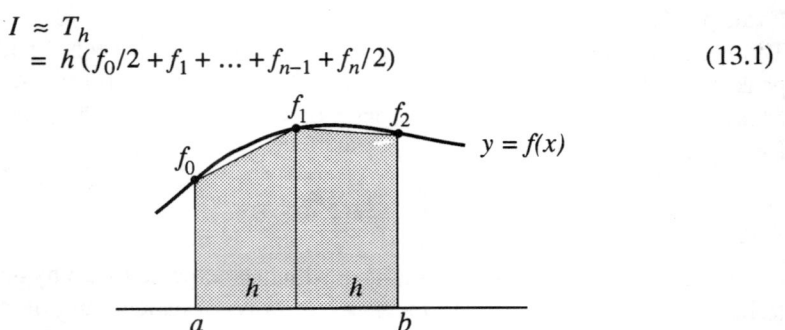

Figure 13.2   The composite trapezoidal rule with n = 2

This is easily implemented as a Pascal function.

```pascal
function Trapint (function f(x:real) : real;
                  a, b : real;  n : integer) : real;
(* Approximates the integral of f(x) from a to b using
   n subintervals in the composite trapezoidal rule *)
    var
        h, sum : real;
        i      : integer;
    begin
    h := (b-a)/n;
    sum := (f(a)+f(b))/2;
    for i := 1 to n-1 do
        sum := sum + f(a+i*h);
    Trapint := h*sum
    end (* Trapint *);
```

We supply the integrand $f(x)$ to Trapint as a *function parameter* (a minority of compilers may require a slightly different syntax for this). The advantage is that Trapint is then self-contained and any function of the specified type can be passed to it as an actual parameter. The alternative would be to omit the function parameter; in that case a function with the specific name f would have to appear before Trapint in the user program.

Application to Example 13.1

We calculate two approximations to the integral

$$I = \int_0^2 x^2 e^{-x^2} dx$$

using the composite trapezoidal rule (13.1) with step sizes 1.0 and 0.5.

x	0.0	0.5	1.0	1.5	2.0
$x^2 e^{-x^2}$	0.0	0.1947	0.3679	0.2371	0.0733

$$T_{1.0} = 1.0 \times (0 + 0.3679 + 0.0733/2) = 0.4046$$
$$T_{0.5} = 0.5 \times (0 + 0.1947 + 0.3679 + 0.2371 + 0.0733/2) = 0.4182$$

Both of these are approximations to I. Presumably $T_{0.5}$ is more accurate than $T_{1.0}$; the question is, how much more accurate?

It can be shown by a somewhat lengthy analysis that the error $E_h = I - T_h$ of the composite trapezoidal rule is approximately proportional to h^2. This means that, if we *halve h*, we get about *four times* the accuracy. Strictly speaking this describes the limiting behaviour as $h \to 0$; if the integrand $f(x)$ has a continuous fourth derivative everywhere in $[a, b]$, then E_h/h^2 tends to a constant as $h \to 0$. Under these conditions we say that the error of the composite trapezoidal rule is $O(h^2)$.

The integrand in example 13.1 more than satisfies the differentiability condition. We write

$$I = T_{1.0} + E_{1.0} = T_{0.5} + E_{0.5}$$

where, in view of the $O(h^2)$ error behaviour,

$$E_{1.0} \approx 4 E_{0.5}$$

We can use this to eliminate $E_{1.0}$ and estimate

$$E_{0.5} \approx (T_{0.5} - T_{1.0})/3$$
$$= (0.4182 - 0.4046)/3 = 0.0045$$

An improved approximation to the integral is then given by

$$I = T_{0.5} + E_{0.5}$$
$$\approx 0.4182 + 0.0045 = 0.4227$$

The important point here is not the numerical result but the idea of *extrapolation*. We have used two different approximations, $T_{1.0}$ and $T_{0.5}$, together with the known limiting behaviour of the error, to obtain an error estimate and hence an improved approximation. This is an example of *Richardson's extrapolation* or *extrapolation to the limit* which can be applied to many similar problems.

13.2 An Automatic Integrator

The calculation at the end of the last section can be summarized as

$$I = T_{h/2} + E_{h/2}$$

where, under certain conditions,

$$E_{h/2} \approx (T_{h/2} - T_h) / 3 \tag{13.2}$$

In a program that employs the composite trapezoidal rule to compute a sequence of values T_h, $T_{h/2}$, $T_{h/4}$, ..., the error can be estimated by this method at every stage and used in a test to terminate the computation when a pre-set accuracy is attained. The user supplies the parameters defining the problem - f, a, b and a tolerance tol (e.g. tol = 0.5e-6 for an accuracy of 6 decimal places) - and the program should do the rest. This is a simple example of an *automatic integrator*.

As a necessary precaution we introduce a *cutoff* on the number of subintervals. This is to ensure that the computation ultimately stops if the integrand is badly behaved or the tolerance is set too small for the computer (an extreme case would be tol = 0.0).

Example 13.2

```
program Integrate (input, output);
(* This program approximates the integral of function fgas(x)
   specified below from x=a to x=b by the composite trapezoidal rule.
   The limits a and b and error tolerance tol are read in as data.
   Extrapolation is used to estimate error bounds and control the
   iteration *)

const
   divisor = 3;        (* for extrapolation of trapezoidal rule *)
   cutoff  = 10000;    (* for number of subintervals *)

var
   n     : integer;
   reply : char;
   a, b, tol, val, oldval, errest : real;
```

```pascal
function fgas (x : real) : real;
(* Specifies the integrand *)
   begin
   fgas := sqr(x)*exp(-sqr(x))
   end;

<function Trapint declared here>

begin (* main program *)
writeln;
writeln('Numerical integration by trapezoidal rule');
writeln('- integrand is specified in the program ...');
writeln;
write('Enter limits of integration:     '); readln(a, b);
repeat
   write('Enter absolute error tolerance:  '); readln(tol);
   n := 2;   val := Trapint(fgas, a, b, n);
   repeat
      oldval := val;
      n := 2*n;
      val := Trapint(fgas, a, b, n);
      errest := (val-oldval)/divisor
   until (abs(errest)<tol) or (n>=cutoff);
   val := val + errest;
   writeln;
   writeln('   Computed approximation = ', val:18);
   writeln('   Estimated error bound   = ', abs(errest):10);
   writeln('   Number of subintervals = ', n);
   if abs(errest) > tol then
      writeln('   WARNING: Required accuracy possibly not attained');
   writeln;
   repeat
      write('Another go for same integral, y or n?  ');
      readln(reply)
   until (reply = 'y') or (reply = 'n');
   writeln
until reply = 'n'
end.
```

Test run:

```
Numerical integration by trapezoidal rule
- integrand is specified in the program ...

Enter limits of integration:     0  2
Enter absolute error tolerance: 0.5e-6
```

```
    Computed approximation =  4.22725056492e-01
    Estimated error bound   =  2.795e-07
    Number of subintervals  =  512
Another go for same integral, y or n?  y

Enter absolute error tolerance:  0.5e-12
    Computed approximation =  4.22725056493e-01
    Estimated error bound   =  2.729e-10
    Number of subintervals  =  16384
    WARNING: Required accuracy possibly not attained
Another go for same integral, y or n?  n
```

[When a very large number of subintervals is used, we should also consider the effects of rounding error on the accuracy of the result - see section 14.2.] Because the step size is continually halved, the integrand will be evaluated more than once at many of the integration points. As function evaluations account for most of the work it is worthwhile economizing, and there is a simple way of doing this (see Exercise Set C).

13.3 Simpson's Rule

We have seen in equation (13.2) how to combine two trapezoidal estimates and produce an improved approximation to an integral. We now derive a formula for this once and for all.

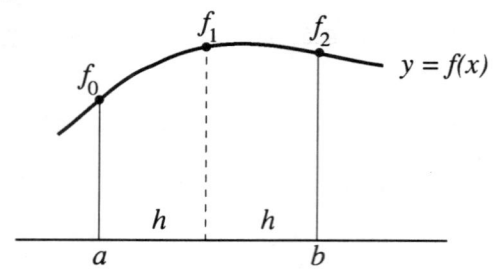

Figure 13.3 For deriving Simpson's rule

Referring to figure 13.3, we write two approximations to the integral of $f(x)$ from a to b,

$$T_{2h} = 2h\,(f_0 + f_2)\,/\,2 = h\,(f_0 + f_2)$$

and

$$T_h = h\,(f_0/2 + f_1 + f_2/2)$$

Following the same scheme as in (13.2) but with renamed step sizes, we derive the improved approximation

$$I \approx T_h + (T_h - T_{2h})/3 = (4T_h - T_{2h})/3$$
$$= h(f_0 + 4f_1 + f_2)/3$$

This is *Simpson's rule*. Another way of obtaining the same formula is to replace the curve $y = f(x)$ by the interpolating quadratic through the three data points and integrate the quadratic instead of $f(x)$ from a to b.

Just as for the trapezoidal rule, we can develop a composite form of Simpson's rule by dividing the range $[a, b]$ into n subintervals of width $h = (b - a)/n$. Clearly, we must now choose n to be *even*. Writing $f_i = f(a + ih)$, $i = 0, 1, \ldots, n$, and summing the basic rule $n/2$ times, we obtain the *composite form of Simpson's rule*,

$$S_h = h(f_0 + 4f_1 + 2f_2 + \ldots + 4f_{n-1} + f_n)/3 \tag{13.3}$$

This can be implemented as a Pascal function.

```
function Simpint (function f(x:real) : real;
                  a, b : real; n : integer) : real;
(* Approximates the integral of f(x) from a to b using
   n subintervals in the composite form of Simpson's rule.
   NOTE: n must be even *)

var
    h, sum  : real;
    i, mult : integer;

begin
h := (b-a)/n;   sum := f(a)+f(b);
mult := 4;
for i := 1 to n-1 do
    begin
    sum := sum + mult*f(a+i*h);
    mult := 6 - mult
    end;
Simpint := (h/3)*sum
end (* Simpint *);
```

It can be shown that, provided the integrand has a continuous sixth-order derivative everywhere in $[a, b]$, the error $E_h = I - S_h$ of composite Simpson's rule is proportional to h^4 as $h \to 0$. This means that, if h is halved, the error decreases in the limit by a factor of $2^4 = 16$. In analogy with the derivation of (13.2), we find

$$I = S_{h/2} + E_{h/2}$$

where, under certain conditions,

$$E_{h/2} \approx (S_{h/2} - S_h) / 15$$

Example 13.3

Simpint can now be slotted into our automatic integrator. The only changes required in program Integrate (example 13.2) are:
(1) replace function Trapint by function Simpint, and invoke Simpint in the main program;
(2) change the constant divisor from 3 to 15 for Simpson's rule;
(3) optionally change trapezoidal to Simpson's throughout, remembering to double the apostrophe in a string.

Test run:

```
Numerical integration by Simpson's rule
- integrand is specified in the program ...

Enter limits of integration:    0  2
Enter absolute error tolerance:  0.5e-6

   Computed approximation =  4.22725058351e-01
   Estimated error bound  =  2.727e-08
   Number of subintervals =  32

Another go for same integral, y or n?  y

Enter absolute error tolerance:  0.5e-12

   Computed approximation =  4.22725056493e-01
   Estimated error bound  =  3.792e-13
   Number of subintervals =  512

Another go for same integral, y or n?  n
```

This should be compared with the earlier output from the program using Trapint. All else being equal, which integrator would you prefer?

Further Developments

If the integrand is sufficiently differentiable, the extrapolation process we have been exploring can be continued as far as desired, with an error estimate available at every stage to control the computation. The general scheme is

$$O(h^2) \quad O(h^4) \quad O(h^6) \quad O(h^8) \quad \cdot \quad \cdot \quad \cdot$$

$$
\begin{array}{ll}
T_h & \\
 & S_{h/2} \\
T_{h/2} & \\
 & S_{h/4} \\
T_{h/4} & \\
 & \cdot \\
\cdot &
\end{array}
$$

The method based on this scheme is called *Romberg integration*.

However, extrapolation is not the answer to all integration problems. By way of warning, we point out that such apparently harmless integrals as

$$\int_{-1}^{1} |x| \, dx, \qquad \int_{0}^{1} \sqrt{1 - x^2} \, dx$$

have discontinuities in the first derivative of the integrand at $x = 0$ and $x = 1$ respectively. Of course we do not need numerical integration for such simple problems. But in cases where we do, there is a class of methods that partition the range $[a, b]$ into subintervals of various sizes and compute an integral over each part separately; where the integrand is 'badly behaved', smaller subintervals can be selected automatically, thus concentrating the effort where it is most needed. These methods, which are conveniently implemented by recursion, are called *adaptive integration schemes*.

14. Numerical Errors

14.1 Error Propagation

Example 14.1

In a design study the formula $f(x) = (1 - x^2)^{-1/2}$ has to be evaluated for an argument $x = \alpha$ that can only be found experimentally. The crucial quantity is measured by the Professor of Futile Engineering in person - $\alpha = 0.98$ correct to 2 decimal places - and the result is confidently calculated as $f(\alpha) = 5.025$. How many figures should we believe?

The answer to this question is surprising, but first we need a little background theory.

Numerical errors (e.g. rounding errors or inexact measurements) in the data supplied to a computational process will *propagate* through to the result. If we want the value of a function f at x but calculate it instead at $x + \delta x$, we need to investigate the difference $\delta f = f(x + \delta x) - f(x)$. It can be shown that, if f is differentiable,

$$\delta f = f'(\xi)\, \delta x$$

where ξ is some point between x and $x + \delta x$ (this is the Mean Value Theorem of calculus). Further, if δx is small and f' is continuous, we can reasonably take $f'(\xi) \approx f'(x)$, so

$$\delta f \approx f'(x)\, \delta x$$

(this seems a long way round to an 'obvious' result, but the conditions are necessary).

In practice we usually know a bound on the error in x, $|\delta x| \le \varepsilon_x$, and we finally arrive at an approximate error bound for f:

$$|\delta f| \le |f'(x)|\, \varepsilon_x \tag{14.1}$$

Application to Example 14.1

It is true that $f(0.98) = 5.025$ to 4 figures. But we want $f(\alpha)$, and $\alpha \neq 0.98$. The professor claims, and we believe her, that the value of α is 0.98 correct to 2 decimal places. This means that the true value satisfies

$$0.975 \leq \alpha < 0.985$$

with the usual rules of rounding. (In general we shall say that an approximation $\bar{x}$ to a real number x is *correct to t decimal places* if $|\bar{x} - x| \leq 0.5 \times 10^{-t}$; in this case $t = 2$.)

In our earlier terminology we have a bound $\varepsilon_x = 0.005$. According to relation (14.1),

$$|\delta f| \leq \frac{|x|}{(1 - x^2)^{3/2}} \varepsilon_x$$

With $x = 0.98$ and $\varepsilon_x = 0.005$, we find

$$|\delta f| \leq 0.622$$

i.e. $\qquad f(\alpha) = 5.025 \pm 0.622$

Every figure of the calculated result may be wrong! (Our estimates are slightly optimistic because of the approximation made in (14.1); the error could be larger.)

Example 14.1 is a case of an *ill-conditioned problem*. In such problems, which unfortunately can arise, small changes in the data are magnified to produce a large change in the solution. Experimental data are always inexact, and rounding errors, unavoidable in calculations with real numbers, make matters worse; in extreme cases the calculated result may be worthless.

There is an extension of the relation (14.1) to functions of more than one variable. For $f(x, y, \ldots)$ we have an (often excessive) error bound

$$|\delta f| \leq |\partial f / \partial x|\, \varepsilon_x + |\partial f / \partial y|\, \varepsilon_y + \ldots$$

We consider two particular cases.

(1) $f(a, b) = a \pm b$. The partial derivatives are both equal to 1, and $|\delta f| \leq \varepsilon_a + \varepsilon_b$.

(2) $f(a, b) = ab$ or a/b . Here it is simpler to take logarithms of absolute values, provided that none of the quantities are zero, before differentiating: $\log |f| = \log |a| \pm \log |b|$, then $|\delta f / f| \leq \varepsilon_a / |a| + \varepsilon_b / |b|$ (note the + sign).

(1) and (2) are often expressed in words as follows (the terms in italics are in effect definitions whose meaning is quite obvious).

(1) The *absolute error* of a sum or difference is bounded by the sum of the *absolute errors* of the arguments.

(2) The *relative error* of a product or quotient is bounded to first approximation by the sum of the *relative errors* of the arguments.

14.2 Machine Numbers

To accommodate as wide a range of real numbers as possible, computers use the *normalized floating-point representation*. Any real number x, other than zero, is represented internally in the form

$$x = f \times 10^m$$

where

$$0.1 \leq |f| < 1.0$$

(computers use a base of 2 or a power of 2 rather than 10, but this and other details need not concern us). Because the exponent m is restricted to a finite range of integers, the real numbers are restricted in absolute value (with a typical maximum of 10^{20} - 10^{40}). Any attempt to generate real numbers on the computer outside this range results in the runtime failure *floating-point overflow*.

The condition on $|f|$ means that f is a signed fraction with first digit nonzero. The fraction has a maximum length of t digits, where t is a constant of the computer called the *precision* (this is actually implementation dependent and some languages provide double or higher precision). Any digits after the first t are rounded according to the usual rules. Thus, taking base 10 and a precision of 4 by way of illustration, we obtain the *machine numbers*

$$4/3 \rightarrow 0.1333 \times 10^1$$
$$8/3 \rightarrow 0.2667 \times 10^1$$

Note that $2 \times (4/3) \neq 8/3$ in this simple model. The implementation on actual computers is more sophisticated, but the moral is that we have to be careful when testing for equality of real numbers or expressions, and this should generally be avoided.

Machine rounding due to finite precision is a source of *rounding error* in practically every step of a computation with real numbers. For example, the arithmetic expression 12.34×2.672 is evaluated on our model computer as

$$12.34 \times 2.672 = (0.1234 \times 10^2) \times (0.2672 \times 10^1)$$
$$= 0.03297248 \times 10^3 \rightarrow 0.3297 \times 10^2$$

The last three figures of the product are lost. Although most computers have a precision equivalent to 8 - 17 decimal digits, and the effect of machine rounding is therefore less, it is still present and can build up in a long computation.

Subtraction of two numbers that are nearly equal leads to a large relative error. Suppose we are solving the quadratic equation $x^2 - 30x + 1 = 0$ by the usual formula, working to 4 figures. We compute the smaller root as

$$15 - (15^2 - 1)^{\frac{1}{2}}$$
$$= 15.00 - 14.97 = 0.03$$

The true value is 0.03337... and the relative error is 10% . What has happened is that most of the leading figures have cancelled out; this is called *extinction* or *cancellation error* (refer to example 6.2 to see how this can be avoided).

Relative Precision

Still working with our 4-decimal digit computer, we add 5×10^{-4} to 1.0. The result is

$$1.0 + 5 \times 10^{-4}$$
$$= 0.1000 \times 10^1 + 0.00005 \times 10^1 \rightarrow 0.1001 \times 10^1$$

The digit 1 appears on the end because of 'rounding up' . Any number smaller than 5×10^{-4} would have no effect when added on to 1.0. This is another curious feature of computer arithmetic: there exist many numbers x for which $1 + x = 1$ even though $x \neq 0$.

The smallest real number u such that $1 + u > 1$ is an important constant of the computer called the *relative precision*. In our example, $u = 5 \times 10^{-4}$. Clearly this is *machine dependent*; we give a program to determine the constant experimentally for any computer.

Example 14.2

```pascal
program RelPrec (output);
(* This program outputs an approximation to the relative precision
   of the computer, determining it experimentally to within a
   factor of 2 *)

var
   u : real;

begin
u := 1;
repeat
   u := u/2
until 1 + u = 1;   (* the final value of u is the relative
                       precision to within a factor of 2 *)
writeln;
write('Relative precision =', 2*u:8);
writeln(' to within a factor of 2')
end.
```

Production run:

```
Relative precision = 2.2e-16 to within a factor of 2
```

We define a constant

```
rprec = 5.0e-16;   (* at least twice the relative precision *)
```

This constant will be required in a number of programs in later chapters. You should find a suitable value for it on your computer by running program RelPrec, or by looking up the system documentation.

The constant rprec is important in the following context. Many iterative processes of numerical computation follow a pattern

```
repeat
    x := x + correction;
    . . . . . . . . .
until abs(correction) < tol
```

where tol is a tolerance parameter set to the required accuracy. Unfortunately, the required accuracy may be unattainable (what would happen if such a program were executed with tol set to 0.0?). The question is, what accuracy is it sensible to ask for?

The smallest correction that can be considered meaningful is the least increment that would have any effect when added on to x. This is given by $u|x|$ where u is the relative precision. It is not useful to seek a correction smaller than this (such quantities are often said to be 'within the roundoff error level'). We therefore can and should make codes of this sort more *robust*, allowing a margin of safety in the good old engineering tradition, by modifying the test to

```
until abs(correction) < tol
    or abs(correction) < rprec*abs(x)
```

14.3 Taylor's Series

Example 14.3
A project student is developing a computer model of an electrical system in which, to represent the current through some of the major components, a function of the form $e^{\lambda t}$ has to be evaluated a great many times. After consulting his supervisor, the student is able to list the following conditions:
(1) the function will only need to be calculated for λt between 0.8 and 1.2;
(2) an accuracy of 3 decimal places is sufficient.
The exp function of Pascal could be used, but this would evaluate $e^{\lambda t}$ to the full precision of the computer (16 figures). This is unnecessary (most of the figures would be meaningless), and the program would run more slowly as a result. How should the student arrange to compute the function?

What is required is an approximation to e^{1+h} that is easy and inexpensive to compute for small h $(-0.2 \leq h \leq 0.2)$; of course we know the value of e^1. This is a special case of a more general problem: given $f(x_0)$, find an approximation to $f(x_0 + h)$ for $h \neq 0$ (in our case $f(x) = e^x$ and $x_0 = 1$).

Consider the quadratic in h,

$$p_2(h) = f_0 + hf_0' + h^2 f_0''/2$$

NOTATION: $f_0 = f(x_0)$, $f_0' = f'(x_0)$, $f_0'' = f''(x_0)$. These are *constants*; the only variable is h. Set h to 0: $p_2(0) = f_0$. Differentiate first with respect to h and then set h to 0: $p_2'(0) = f_0'$. Differentiate twice with respect to h and set h to 0: $p_2''(0) = f_0''$. We conclude that the quadratic p_2 agrees with the function f in its zeroth, first and second derivatives, all evaluated at x_0.

Similarly the polynomial of degree n in h,

$$p_n(h) = f_0 + hf_0' + h^2 f_0''/2! + \ldots + h^n f_0^{(n)}/n!$$

can be shown to match the function f in its zeroth, first, ..., nth derivatives all at x_0 (provided, of course, f has sufficient derivatives). Let us try this out for $f(x) = \sin x$ with $x_0 = 0$. We obtain

$$f_0 = \sin 0 = 0, \quad f_0' = \cos 0 = 1,$$
$$f_0'' = -\sin 0 = 0, \quad f_0''' = -\cos 0 = -1, \quad \text{etc.}$$

Writing x for h (since $x_0 + h$ now reduces to h), we find that the polynomial is

$$p_n(x) = x - x^3/3! + x^5/5! - \ldots + (-1)^{(n-1)/2} x^n/n!$$

where n may be $1, 3, 5, \ldots$.

We regard the polynomial $p_n(h)$ as an infinite series truncated at the term in h^n. Introducing a remainder or error term $R_n(h)$, we write (see figure 14.1)

$$f(x_0 + h) = f_0 + hf_0' + h^2 f_0''/2! + \ldots + h^n f_0^{(n)}/n! + R_n(h) \qquad (14.2)$$

This is the *truncated Taylor's series with remainder* for the expansion of $f(x_0 + h)$ about x_0. It is the basis of all the familiar (?) series for e^x, $\sin x$, etc.

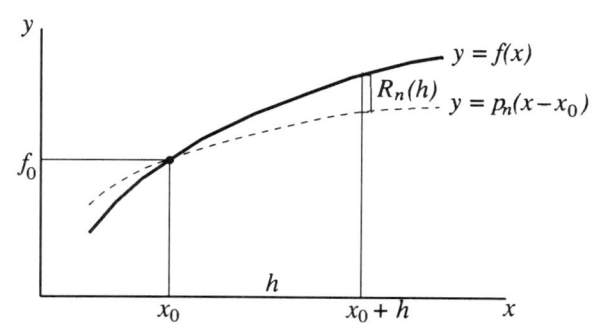

Figure 14.1 The problem addressed by Taylor's series

Our intention is to evaluate the polynomial $p_n(h)$ and use it to approximate $f(x_0 + h)$ for a given function f. In order to make use of the truncated Taylor's series in this way, we need some information on the size of the *truncation error* $R_n(h)$. This is provided by the following theorem, which is proved in most textbooks of calculus.

Theorem 14.1 (Taylor's Theorem)

If the function $f(x)$ has an $(n+1)$st derivative, denoted by $f^{(n+1)}(x)$, everywhere from x_0 to $x_0 + h$, then the error of the approximating polynomial $p_n(h)$ is

$$R_n(h) = \frac{h^{n+1}}{(n+1)!} f^{(n+1)}(\xi)$$

where ξ is an unknown point lying between x_0 and $x_0 + h$.

Application to Example 14.3

Taking $f(x) = e^x$ and $x_0 = 1$, we find that $f_0 = f_0' = f_0'' = \ldots = e$. From equation (14.2) and Theorem 14.1,

$$f(1 + h) = (1 + h + h^2/2! + \ldots + h^n/n!)\, e + h^{n+1} e^{\xi}/(n+1)!$$

For an accuracy of 3 decimal places we must choose n so that, when $|h| \leq 0.2$, the truncation error is guaranteed to be less than 0.5×10^{-3}. Since ξ is known to lie between 1 and $1 + h$, the worst possible case that might arise would be $h = 0.2$, $\xi = 1.2$, giving

$$|\text{error}| < 0.2^{n+1}\, e^{1.2}/(n+1)!$$

For $n = 1, 2, 3$ this error bound is 0.0664, 0.0044, 0.0002. It is therefore sufficient to take $n = 3$, and we may use the approximate formula

$$e^{1+h} \approx (1 + h + h^2/2 + h^3/6) \times 2.7183$$

For example,

$$e^{0.9} \approx (1 - 0.1 + 0.01/2 - 0.001/6) \times 2.7183$$
$$= 2.4596 \text{ correct to at least 3 decimal places.}$$

Approximations to Derivatives

The formulae (14.3) and (14.4) to be derived below will be used for the numerical solution of certain types of differential equation in chapter 18.

Suppose that the function $f(x)$ is three times differentiable in the interval $(x_0 - h, x_0 + h)$, then

$$f(x_0 + h) = f_0 + hf_0' + h^2 f_0''/2 + h^3 f'''(\xi_1)/6, \quad x_0 < \xi_1 < x_0 + h,$$
$$f(x_0 - h) = f_0 - hf_0' + h^2 f_0''/2 - h^3 f'''(\xi_2)/6, \quad x_0 - h < \xi_2 < x_0.$$

By subtracting these two equations and solving for f_0', we obtain a formula that can be used to approximate the first derivative of f at x_0,

$$f'(x_0) = \frac{f(x_0+h) - f(x_0-h)}{2h} + O(h^2) \tag{14.3}$$

The notation $O(h^2)$ (read 'order h squared') means that the error $E(h)$ of the approximation satisfies

$$|E(h)| \leq M h^2$$

where M is a constant independent of h. (It is sufficient here if f''' is bounded in $(x_0 - h, x_0 + h)$.) Under these conditions we say that (14.3) is an $O(h^2)$ approximation to $f'(x_0)$. In general, the higher the order of approximation, the more rapidly the error decreases as $h \to 0$, and we expect to obtain higher accuracy for less computational effort. The drawback is that the function has to be 'sufficiently differentiable', that is, the derivative appearing in the error term must exist and be bounded.

By extending the two series above to the terms in h^4, and assuming that the fourth derivative of f is bounded in $(x_0 - h, x_0 + h)$, we can quite easily obtain an important approximation for the second derivative,

$$f''(x_0) = \frac{f(x_0+h) - 2f(x_0) + f(x_0-h)}{h^2} + O(h^2) \tag{14.4}$$

Exercise Set C

11.1 A radioactive isotope decays according to the law $m = m_0 e^{-\lambda t}$. The mass of isotope present in a given sample can be inferred from the intensity of radiation. The following values are recorded:

time (hours)	1	2	3	4	5	6	7	8
mass (grams)	3.92	3.01	2.28	1.94	1.37	1.11	0.89	0.72

Find an approximate value for the decay constant λ, and hence estimate the *half-life* of the isotope (the time it takes for half a given amount to decay).

11.2 Show how to linearize the problem of fitting a curve $y = Ax^b$ to a set of data points (x_i, y_i), $i = 1, \ldots, m$, by least squares. Find a curve of this type that best fits the data

x	1	3	5	6	8	10
y	1.43	2.69	3.71	4.13	4.82	5.63

11.3 The equation of a plane through the origin in three dimensions is given by $z = ax + by$, where a and b are constants. Show how to fit such a plane to a set of data points (x_i, y_i, z_i), $i = 1, \ldots, m$, by the least squares method, assuming the deviations to be in the z direction, and derive the normal equations.

Modify program LineFit (example 11.2) to compute the a and b values for this problem. Test on the data

x	1	−1	−2	4	−6
y	1	1	4	2	2
z	2	1	5	5	0.1

(these points lie almost exactly on a plane through the origin).

11.4 The system of equations

$$x - 2y = -1.04, \qquad 3x - y = 1.96$$
$$2x + 3y = 5.07, \qquad x + 4y = 4.93$$

is said to be *overdetermined*. Any pair of the equations can be solved for x and y, but the resulting solution will not satisfy the remaining equations. By the principle of least squares we can find a 'solution' which, while not satisfying any equation exactly, best satisfies the system as a whole. Show that this problem is equivalent to that already discussed in exercise 11.3 (with different names for the unknowns). Hence find best values for x and y in the least squares sense.

12.1 For function values $f_0, f_1, f_2, \ldots$ at *equally-spaced* nodes $x_0, x_1, x_2, \ldots$ (i.e. constant stepwidth $h = x_1 - x_0 = x_2 - x_1 = \ldots$), an array of the form

$$
\begin{array}{ll}
f_0 \\
f_1 & f_1 - f_0 \\
f_2 & f_2 - f_1 & (f_2 - f_1) - (f_1 - f_0) \\
\cdot \cdot \cdot \cdot \cdot \cdot \cdot \cdot \cdot \cdot \cdot \cdot \cdot \cdot \cdot \cdot \cdot \cdot \cdot \cdot \cdot \cdot \cdot \cdot \cdot
\end{array}
$$

is called a *difference table*. Write a program to output the difference table for a set of function values $f_0, f_1, f_2, \ldots, f_n$, and test on the data

x	1.1	1.2	1.3	1.4	1.5
$\log_e x$	0.0953	0.1823	0.2624	0.3365	0.4055

12.2 The entries $f_1 - f_0$ and $f_2 - 2f_1 + f_0$ in a difference table are called *first* and *second forward differences* of f_0, denoted by Δf_0 and $\Delta^2 f_0$ respectively. Consider an arbitrary argument x, expressed in terms of x_0 and the stepwidth h as $x = x_0 + \theta h$ (for example, if $0 < \theta < 1$ then x lies between x_0 and x_1). Show that the quadratic

$$p_2(\theta) = f_0 + \theta \Delta f_0 + \theta(\theta - 1)\Delta^2 f_0 / 2$$

interpolates $f(x)$ at the first three data points (check values of $p_2(\theta)$ at $\theta = 0, 1, 2$).
It can be proved that the polynomial of degree n

$$p_n(\theta) = f_0 + \theta \Delta f_0 + \ldots + \theta(\theta - 1) \ldots (\theta - n + 1)\Delta^n f_0 / n!$$

interpolates $f(x)$ at the first $n + 1$ data points. The interpolating polynomial in this form is called *Newton's forward formula*. Use it to find the most accurate values you can for $\log_e 1.15$ and $\log_e 1.23$ from the data in exercise 12.1.

12.3 (i) For a given set of data points (x_i, f_i), $i = 0, \ldots, n$, function Lagrange (example 12.2) returns the value of the interpolating polynomial $p_n(x)$ at $x = \bar{x}$. Write a program to tabulate $p_n(x)$ at equally-spaced arguments over an interval $[a, b]$. Use the program to tabulate the interpolant of cos x on the node set $-90°, -60°, 0, 60°, 90°, 120°, 180°, 240°, 270°$ at steps of $10°$ over $[-90°, 270°]$.

(ii) If you have access to a computer graphics facility, plot the points tabulated in part (i). Also draw the graph of the Pascal function cos and see how closely the curves match.

12.4 Write a program that calls procedure Neville (example 12.3) to compute an approximation to $f(\bar{x})$, given a set of data points (x_i, f_i), $i = 0, \ldots, n$, and an argument $\bar{x}$. Use the program to find an approximation to sin 60° based on the values of sin x at $x = -90°, -30°, 0, 30°, 90°$. Output the 'estimated error bound'. Do you believe it? Display the Neville table to see what has happened.

13.1 Develop a version of the automatic integrator (example 13.2) with Trapint replaced by Simpint as described in section 13.3. Use it to approximate the integral

$$\int_0^1 \frac{4}{1 + x^2} \, dx \quad (= \pi)$$

Hence calculate π as accurately as your computer permits.

13.2 If approximations T_h and $T_{h/2}$ are calculated by the composite trapezoidal rule, the new points for $T_{h/2}$ are equally spaced between the original points for T_h. Show that

$$T_{h/2} = T_h/2 + D(h)$$

where $D(h)$ depends only on the new integration points, and obtain an expression for $D(h)$.

   If this idea is used in an automatic integrator with the trapezoidal rule, the amount of computation can be approximately halved. Modify function Trapint to do this. The function will require an extra parameter to supply the old value T_h. Test the modified automatic integrator on the problems of example 13.2 and exercise 13.1.

13.3 An odd periodic function $f(x)$ of period 2π can be expressed under quite general conditions as a *Fourier sine series*

$$f(x) = \sum_{m=1}^{\infty} d_m \sin mx$$

where

$$d_m = \frac{2}{\pi} \int_0^{\pi} f(x) \sin mx \, dx$$

Write a program based on the automatic integrator of exercise 13.1 to compute the Fourier coefficients $d_1, \ldots, d_M$ for such a function. Test on the periodic sawtooth function defined by $f(x) = x$ for $-\pi < x < \pi$, $f(\pi) = 0$ and $f(x + 2\pi k) = f(x)$ for any integer k. Compute the coefficients $d_1, \ldots, d_{10}$ as accurately as possible (you should be able to calculate these by hand as a check).

14.1 The values of two variables x and y are subject to small uncertainties bounded by ε_x and ε_y respectively. Derive error bounds for

$$\pi x y^2, \qquad x \log_e y, \qquad x^y$$

to first order in ε_x and ε_y.

The values of x and y are given as $x = 12.42$, $y = 1.764$, both correct to 4 figures. Evaluate the three functions above and state how many figures can be claimed correct in each result.

14.2 The truncated Taylor's series for sin x has been developed in section 14.3. The truncation error is bounded by the absolute value of the first neglected term in the series (can you show this by Theorem 14.1?) Write a function sine(x, tol) to compute sin x to an accuracy tol by this method. Use it to find sin x correct to 6 decimal places for values of x in the interval $[-\pi/2, \pi/2]$, and compare with the Pascal function sin.

14.3 Develop and improve function sine from exercise 14.2 as follows.

(i) For large x (say $x = 1000$) many terms would be required for convergence, and in practice there would be problems of overflow and cancellation error. Devise a way round this using the periodicity of the sine function.

(ii) Dispense with the parameter tol and compute sin x to full machine accuracy (for ideas on this see section 14.2).

Test the resulting code against the Pascal function sin for a wide range of positive and negative arguments.

Part 4

Solution of Equations

15. Nonlinear Equations

Example 15.1

The Emir Abdul el Bulbul has learned that certain infidel *magi* of the west are able to figure the mystical Seventh Root of Seven correct even unto the seventh place. Determined to procure this secret, he orders the Grand Vizier to seek such a one in the four quarters, decreeing a reward of twelve score and twelve camels tax-free, subject to the usual small print.

The mathematician of chapter 12, now on his way home and still without his calculator, finds himself summoned for this task. How can he save his head?

15.1 The Bisection Method

Given a real-valued function $f(x)$, we call any number α that satisfies $f(\alpha) = 0$ a *root* of the equation $f(x) = 0$ or a *zero* of f. In general there may be none, one or many, and the roots may be real or complex.

Suppose we can find an interval $[a, b]$ (for example by tabulating $f(x)$, sketching the curve or using a graph-plotting routine) such that f is continuous and changes sign from a to b (a simple test for this is $f(a)f(b) < 0$). Then there is at least one real root α of $f(x) = 0$ in $[a, b]$.

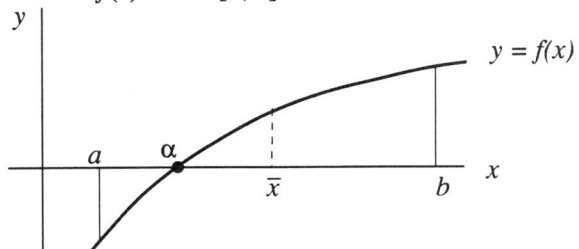

Figure 15.1 One step of the bisection method

Denoting the mid point of $[a, b]$ by $\bar{x} = (a+b)/2$, we deduce that there is a root in either $[a, \bar{x}]$ or $[\bar{x}, b]$ (possibly both). We can halve the interval known to contain a root by moving up a or b as follows:

if $f(\bar{x})f(b) > 0$ **then**
  $b := \bar{x}$
else
  $a := \bar{x}$

The same process can be continued with the new $[a, b]$, and so on apparently indefinitely. This is the *bisection method*.

Application to Example 15.1

An nth root of c is a solution of $x^n - c = 0$. In the present case $c = 7$, $n = 7$, and the mathematician rather urgently wants a real root. An obvious starting interval is $[1.0, 1.5]$. Then

iteration number	$\bar{x}$
1	1.25
2	1.375
.	.
.	.
.	.
20	1.32046938

At this stage the width of the interval is $0.5/2^{20} = 0.48 \times 10^{-6}$, and the root may be any point between 1.32046890 and 1.32046938. Thus $7^{1/7} = 1.320469$ correct to 7 figures.

Example 15.2

Write a program to find a root of $f(x) = 0$ by the bisection method, provided a suitable starting interval can be found, and use it to solve the equation $x = e^{-x}$ correct to 8 decimal places.

A sketch and calculation suggests that there is a single root in $[0.0, 1.0]$.

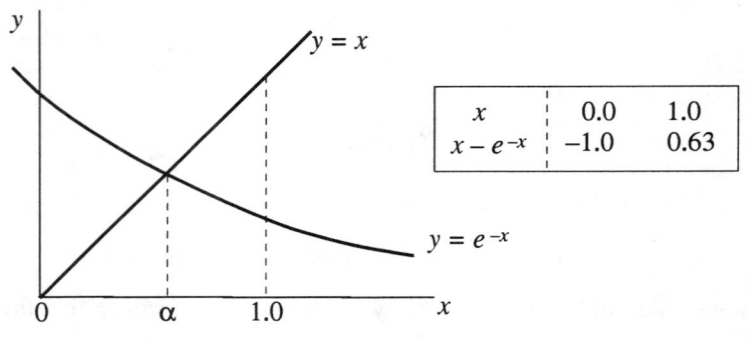

x	0.0	1.0
$x - e^{-x}$	-1.0	0.63

Figure 15.2   To solve $x = e^{-x}$

```
program Bisection (input, output);
(* This program finds a root of f(x)=0, for function f below,
   by the bisection method. An initial interval over which f(x)
   changes sign and an error tolerance tol are read in as data *)

const
   rprec = 5.0e-16;      (* machine-dependent constant, at least twice
                            the relative precision of the computer *)
var
   a, b, x, fa, fb, fx, tol : real;
   iter : integer;

function f (x : real) : real;
(* Specifies the equation to be solved, f(x)=0 *)
   begin
   f := x - exp(-x)
   end;

begin  (* main program *)
writeln;
writeln('Solution of nonlinear equation by bisection method');
writeln('- equation is specified in the program ...');
writeln;
write('Enter initial interval  a  b  : '); readln(a, b);
write('Enter absolute error tolerance: '); readln(tol);
writeln;

fa := f(a); fb := f(b);
if fa*fb >0 then
   writeln('ERROR: Function does not change sign')
else
   begin  (* bisection method starting with [a,b] *)
   iter := 0;
   repeat
      iter := iter+1;
      x := a+(b-a)/2; fx := f(x); (* evaluate function at mid point *)
      if fx*fb >0 then
         begin  (* root lies in [a,x] *)
         b := x; fb := fx
         end
      else
         begin  (* root lies in [x,b] *)
         a := x; fa := fx
         end
   until (abs(b-a)<tol) or (abs(b-a)<rprec*abs(x));
```

```
    writeln('Computed root = ', x:20);
    writeln('Number of iterations =', iter:4)
    end
end.
```

Notes:
(1) The program is organized so that only one evaluation of *f* is required at each iteration (function evaluations are by far the most expensive element of the computation).
(2) The mid point is computed by adding a correction on to *a*, x := a+(b-a)/2, which is preferable when the interval width approaches the roundoff error level.
(3) The machine-dependent constant rprec discussed in section 14.2 is used to back up the convergence test; the program will work for any value of tol, including 0.

Test runs:

```
Solution of nonlinear equation by bisection method
- equation is specified in the program ...

Enter initial interval  a  b  :  0.0  0.5
Enter absolute error tolerance:  0.5e-8
ERROR: Function does not change sign


Solution of nonlinear equation by bisection method
- equation is specified in the program ...

Enter initial interval  a  b  :  0.5  1.0
Enter absolute error tolerance:  0.5e-8
Computed root =  5.6714328750968e-01
Number of iterations =  27
```

15.2 Newton's Method

The Emir is not greatly impressed with the bisection method. Although, under the stated conditions, it is guaranteed to find a root - the mathematician claims it is *robust* - it takes a long time, and His Effluence is not noted for patience. Can one do better?

Suppose we have an initial approximation x_0 to a root α of $f(x) = 0$. If a tangent is fitted to the curve $y = f(x)$ at $x = x_0$, this will intersect the *x*-axis at some point x_1 (provided the gradient of the tangent is nonzero).

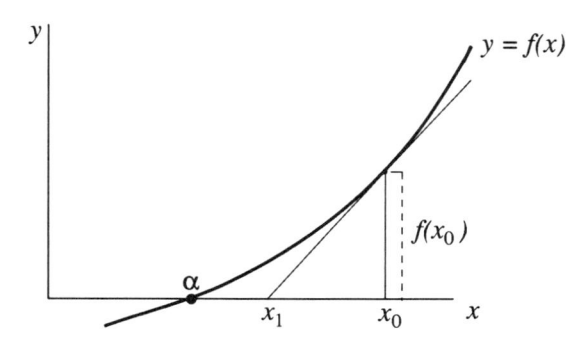

Figure 15.3 One step of Newton's method

The point x_1 appears to be a closer approximation to α than x_0 (at least if the curve behaves as in the figure!). We can find x_1 as follows:

$$\frac{f(x_0)}{x_0 - x_1} = \text{gradient of tangent at } x_0$$
$$= f'(x_0)$$

which can be solved for x_1 to give

$$x_1 = x_0 - f(x_0)/f'(x_0)$$

The process can be repeated with x_1 etc, giving an iterative scheme

$$x_{k+1} = x_k - f(x_k)/f'(x_k), \qquad k = 0,1, \ldots \tag{15.1}$$

This is *Newton's method.*

An important property of Newton's method is that it satisfies a *local convergence theorem*: if the starting value x_0 is sufficiently close to α, then, under fairly mild conditions on f, the sequence $x_0, x_1, \ldots$ converges to α. This is far from saying that Newton's method will always work; the significance of 'sufficiently close' depends on particular cases.

Application to Example 15.1

We have $f(x) = x^n - c$, $f'(x) = nx^{n-1}$, and

$$x - \frac{f(x)}{f'(x)} = x - \frac{x^n - c}{nx^{n-1}} = \frac{1}{n}\left((n-1)x + c/x^{n-1}\right)$$

With $c = 7$, $n = 7$, the iteration is

$$x_{k+1} = (6/7)\,x_k + (1/x_k)^6$$

Taking a starting value of $x_0 = 1.5$, we find

$$x_1 = \underline{1.3}73\ 505\ 78$$
$$x_2 = \underline{1.3}26\ 232\ 62$$
$$x_3 = \underline{1.320}\ 543\ 84$$
$$x_4 = \underline{1.320\ 469\ 2}6$$
$$x_5 = \underline{1.320\ 469\ 25}$$

The figures which are correct at each stage are underlined. The next correction would be much smaller than 10^{-6}, so x_5 (and in fact x_4) are correct to 7 figures. (You might see what happens if you start with $x_0 = 0.5$ instead.)

Application to Example 15.2

We give a program to seek a root of $f(x) = 0$ by Newton's method, using it to solve $x = e^{-x}$ with starting value $x_0 = 1.0$ (see figure 15.2).

```
program Newton (input, output);
(* This program attempts to find a root of f(x)=0, for function f
   below, by Newton's method. A derivative function fd is required.
   The starting value and error tolerance are read in as data *)

const
   maxiter = 20;      (* cutoff in case of failure to converge *)
   rprec   = 5.0e-16; (* at least twice the relative precision *)

var
   x, tol, correction : real;
   iter               : integer;
   converged          : boolean;

function f (x : real) : real;
(* Specifies the equation to be solved, f(x)=0 *)
   begin
   f := x - exp(-x)
   end;

function fd (x : real) : real;
(* Specifies the derivative f'(x) *)
   begin
   fd := 1 + exp(-x)
   end;

begin  (* main program *)
writeln('Solution of nonlinear equation by Newton''s method');
writeln('- equation is specified in the program ...');
writeln;
write('Enter initial approximation  : '); readln(x);
write('Enter absolute error tolerance: '); readln(tol);
writeln;
```

```
iter := 0;
repeat
   correction := -f(x)/fd(x);
   x := x + correction;
   writeln('     ', x:20);
   converged := (abs(correction) < tol)  or
               (abs(correction) < rprec*abs(x));
   iter := iter+1
until converged or (iter = maxiter);

writeln;
if converged then
   writeln('Computed root = ', x:20)
else
   writeln('Newton''s method fails to converge in ',
          maxiter:2, ' iterations');
writeln
end.
```

Test run:

```
Solution of nonlinear equation by Newton's method
- equation is specified in the program ...

Enter initial approximation   :  1.0
Enter absolute error tolerance:  0.5e-8

      5.3788284273999e-01
      5.6698699140541e-01
      5.6714328598912e-01
      5.6714329040978e-01

Computed root =  5.6714329040978e-01
```

Robustness

Although, close to a root, Newton's method normally converges much more rapidly than the bisection method, it is inferior in one very important respect: it does not possess guaranteed convergence. The sequence of iterates produced by equation (15.1) may *diverge*, which is why we have included a cutoff of 20 iterations in program Newton. The program may still fail catastrophically; this is best illustrated by an example.

Example 15.3
The equation $1 + 3/x^2 - 4/x^3 = 0$ has a single root at $x = 1$. We attempt to find this root by Newton's method with two different starting values, $x_0 = 1.3$ and $x_0 = 3.0$.

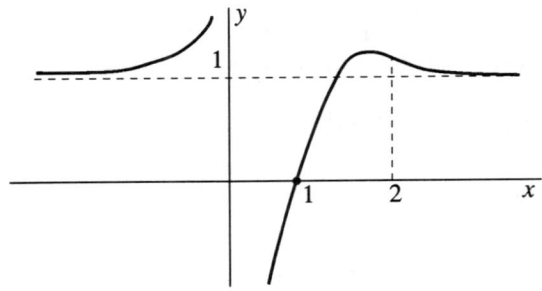

Figure 15.4 Graph of $y = 1 + 3/x^2 - 4/x^3$

We modify the functions f and fd in program Newton and execute the program.

Test runs:

```
Solution of nonlinear equation by Newton's method
- equation is specified in the program ...
Enter initial approximation   :  1.3
Enter absolute error tolerance:  0.5e-8
        6.5092857142857e-01
        7.9337986204724e-01
        9.1616847906272e-01
        9.8414441938663e-01
        9.9938391662391e-01
        9.9999905184320e-01
        9.9999999999775e-01
        1.0000000000000e+00
Computed root =  1.0000000000000e+00


Solution of nonlinear equation by Newton's method
- equation is specified in the program ...
Enter initial approximation   :  3.0
Enter absolute error tolerance:  0.5
        1.9000000000000e+01
        1.3065294117647e+03
        3.7228361644539e+08
        8.5994470006119e+24
```

Execution stopped: floating-point overflow

It should be clear from figure 15.4 what has happened: in the second case the starting value is not 'sufficiently close' to the root and the iterates diverge. In general, this requirement is difficult to formulate and virtually impossible to test in a program. If the algorithm can lead to overflow after four iterations, we cannot claim that it is a reliable method for solving general nonlinear equations. In fact Newton's method has two major drawbacks for automatic computation:
(1) The sequence of iterates may diverge if the starting value is not close enough to a root, and there are cases where runtime failure is difficult to prevent.
(2) The derivative $f'(x)$ is required, so $f(x)$ must be reasonably easy to differentiate and the resulting function not overly expensive to compute ($f'(x)$ has to be evaluated at every iteration).

In the next section we shall see how a start can be made on overcoming these problems.

15.3 The Secant Method

If we make use of two points on the curve, we can replace the tangent in Newton's method by a secant.

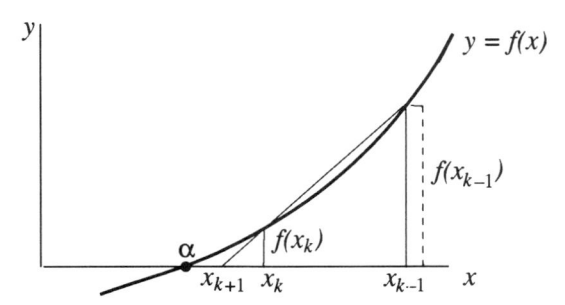

Figure 15.5   One step of the secant method

In equation (15.1), $f'(x_k)$ is replaced by the gradient of the secant,

$$g_k = \frac{f(x_{k-1}) - f(x_k)}{x_{k-1} - x_k}$$

giving the iterative scheme

$$x_{k+1} = x_k - f(x_k)/g_k, \qquad k = 1, 2, \ldots$$

This is the *secant method*. Initially, two points x_0 and x_1 are required together with their function values, but the computation can be organized so that only one evaluation of f is necessary at each subsequent step. The derivative is not involved at all.

We give a procedure for this method (note outcome (3) in the procedure description: the secant method suffers from the same erratic behaviour as Newton's method).

Example 15.4

```pascal
procedure Secant (function f(x:real) : real;  x0, xl, tol : real;
                  trace : boolean;
                  var root : real;  var converged : boolean);
(* This procedure attempts to find a root of f(x)=0 by the secant
   method. Two starting values must be supplied in x0 and xl and
   an absolute error tolerance in tol. If the procedure is called
   with trace set to true, intermediate iterates are written to
   the output file as a diagnostic aid. The computation terminates
   in one of three ways:
   (1) convergence is attained and the computed value is returned
   in root with converged set to true;
   (2) convergence is not attained after maxiter iterations - the
   latest value is returned in root with converged set to false;
   (3) under certain conditions a runtime failure may occur arising
   from real overflow or attempted zero division *)
const
   maxiter = 20;    (* maximum number of iterations allowed *)
   rprec = 5.0e-16; (* machine-dependent constant, at least twice
                       the relative precision of the computer *)
var
   f0, fl, correction : real;
   iter : integer;

begin
iter := 0; f0 := f(x0);
repeat
   fl :=f(xl);
   (* Compute correction to xl by secant method *)
   correction := -fl*((x0-xl)/(f0-fl));
   x0 := xl; f0 := fl;    (* save latest estimate *)
   xl := xl + correction; (* compute new estimate *)
   if trace then
      writeln(xl:20);
   converged := (abs(correction) < tol) or
                (abs(correction) < rprec*abs(xl));
   iter := iter+1
until converged or (iter = maxiter);
root := xl
end (* Secant *);
```

The minimum requirements for a robust and efficient algorithm to solve nonlinear equations in one variable may now be stated as:
(1) guaranteed convergence to a real root, given a starting interval of the type discussed in section 15.1;
(2) rapid convergence close to a root;
(3) only one function evaluation per step, and no derivative requirement.
These criteria can be met by a combination of the bisection and secant methods. Broadly speaking, the role of bisection is to refine the interval until the secant method can take over and give final rapid convergence. The root is bracketed by known values at every stage, so there are no problems of divergence.

Bisection/Secant Algorithm

To compute a real root of $f(x) = 0$ in an interval $[a, b]$ over which f is continuous and changes sign:

Initialization
　$x_0 = a,\ \ x_1 = b,\ \ f_0 = f(x_0),\ \ f_1 = f(x_1)$
repeat
　　set $g = (f_0 - f_1) / (x_0 - x_1)$　　　　{ gradient of secant }
　　set $x_0 = x_1,\ f_0 = f_1$　　　　　　{ save latest values }
　　if $g \neq 0$ **then**
　　　set $x_1 = x_1 - f_1 / g$　　　　　　{ try a secant step }
　　if x_1 not in (a, b) **or** $g = 0$ **then**
　　　set $x_1 = a + (b - a)/2$　　　　{ use bisection instead }
　　{ now $a < x_1 < b$ }
　　evaluate $f_1 = f(x_1)$
　　use $x_1,\ f_1$ to reduce $[a, b]$ as in bisection method
until $|b - a|$ within tolerance **or** $f_1 = 0$

output x_1　　　　　　　　　　　{ approximation to root }

Conditions such as $g = 0$ and $f_1 = 0$ need some elaboration. A consequence of the floating-point representation of real numbers (see section 14.2) is that there is a *smallest positive real number* representable on the computer, typically in the range 10^{-20} - 10^{-40}. Let us call this minreal (its value could be found experimentally by a program similar to MaxReal in section 2.3). The 'real zero' of the computer then corresponds to a range of mathematical real numbers, namely all those which are smaller in absolute value than minreal. Tests comparing real quantities with zero have to take account of this, with a margin allowed for safety.

Further Developments

Newton's method can be extended, at least in principle, to solve a system of n simultaneous nonlinear equations in n variables, of which a simple example is

$$\begin{cases} \pi\, e^x + 6y = 0 \\ 2\sin(x+y) + 1 = 0 \end{cases}$$

In general, a major difficulty is the amount of computation involved; it turns out that each iterative step requires n^2 function evaluations and the solution of an $n \times n$ system of linear equations, which tends to restrict the applicability to small systems. Modifications of Newton's method and the secant method have been devised which, while usually giving slower convergence, significantly reduce the computational cost per step.

With any iterative method for systems there is the problem of finding a sufficiently close initial approximation to a solution, or indeed locating a solution at all, since the interval approach we have described for single equations is obviously not applicable.

16. Polynomials

Example 16.1
Polynomials of degree 3 or higher occur in many applications; their zeros may be real or complex. For example, the cubic

$$p_3(x) = x^3 - 12x + 7$$

has three real zeros, as can be seen by sketching the curve $y = p_3(x)$ or using a graph-plotting routine. Is there any direct method (perhaps on the lines of the quadratic formula) for solving cubic equations such as $p_3(x) = 0$? How should one go about computing the zeros of polynomials in general?

Before we can answer this, we must first decide on a suitable way of evaluating polynomials.

16.1 Evaluation of Polynomials

At first sight it appears that there is no problem about calculating the value of a polynomial

$$p_n(x) = a_n x^n + \ldots + a_1 x + a_0$$

for any given x, because the process is a finite one involving only the operations of multiplication and addition. However, a little thought shows that the naive method of substituting for x directly into the terms of the polynomial is by no means the best (the same powers of x would have to be calculated many times over unless intermediate results were saved in some way).

We can do better than this. Referring to example 16.1, we write the cubic in *nested form* as

$$p_3(x) = ((1x + 0)x - 12)x + 7$$

(we start by placing the coefficient of the highest power of x in the innermost parentheses and work outwards, not forgetting the term $0x^2$). Suppose we want to evaluate $p_3(x)$ at $x = 3$. We can do this with the nested form by calculating

$$b_2 = 1 \qquad\qquad\qquad : \qquad 1$$
$$b_1 = b_2 \times 3 + 0 \;\; = \;\; 3 \qquad : \qquad 1x + 0$$
$$b_0 = b_1 \times 3 - 12 = -3 \qquad : \qquad (1x + 0)x - 12$$
$$b_{-1} = b_0 \times 3 + 7 \;\; = -2 \qquad : \qquad ((1x + 0)x - 12)x + 7$$
$$= p_3(3) \tag{16.1}$$

This is *Horner's scheme*. The reason for the b_i notation will appear shortly.

If we are only interested in the final value, the method is very easy to program; for a polynomial of degree n we have

```
b := a[n];
for i := n-1 downto 0 do
    b := b*x + a[i];
(* final value of b is the value of the polynomial *)
```

Apart from its convenience for programming, the method is also most efficient, requiring only n multiplications and n additions (the naive method would require around $n^2/2$ multiplications and n additions).

Extended Horner's Scheme

The results of the calculation (16.1) for $p_3(x)$ at $x = 3$ can be expressed as

$$x^3 - 12x + 7 = (x - 3)(x^2 + 3x - 3) - 2$$
$$= (x - 3)(b_2 x^2 + b_1 x + b_0) + b_{-1}$$

This can be verified by comparing the coefficients of powers of x on both sides. In general, if Horner's scheme is used to evaluate $p_n(x)$ at $x = \bar{x}$, and the numbers $b_{n-1}, \ldots, b_0, b_{-1}$ are produced, it can be shown that

$$p_n(x) = (x - \bar{x})(b_{n-1} x^{n-1} + \ldots + b_0) + b_{-1} \tag{16.2}$$

Writing this as

$$p_n(x) = (x - \bar{x})q_{n-1}(x) + b_{-1}$$

and differentiating with respect to x, we find

$$p_n'(x) = q_{n-1}(x) + (x - \bar{x})q_{n-1}'(x)$$

Finally, setting $x = \bar{x}$,

$$p_n'(\bar{x}) = q_{n-1}(\bar{x})$$

The remarkable result is that the *derivative* $p_n'(\bar{x})$ can be calculated by evaluating the polynomial $q_{n-1}(x)$ at $x = \bar{x}$. For this a second application of Horner's scheme may be used. In our example,

$$q_2(x) = x^2 + 3x - 3$$
$$= (1x + 3)x - 3$$

then at $x = 3$,

$$c_1 = 1,$$
$$c_0 = c_1 \times 3 + 3 = 6$$
$$c_{-1} = c_0 \times 3 - 3 = 15$$
$$= p_3'(3)$$

We summarize this in a Pascal procedure which will be immediately useful. The following data types are assumed:

```
degree = 0..maxdeg;
coeffs = array[degree] of real;
```

```
procedure Horner (n : degree;  var a : coeffs;  x : real;
                  var val, grad : real);
(* This procedure evaluates the polynomial
        p(x) = a[n]x^n + ... + a[1]x + a[0]
   and its derivative p'(x) for a specified argument x using
   extended Horner's scheme. The values of p(x) and p'(x) are
   returned in val and grad *)

var
    b, c : real;
    i    : degree;
begin
b := a[n];   c := 0;
(* b accumulates the value p(x),
   c accumulates the value p'(x) *)
for i := n-1 downto 0 do
    begin
    c := c*x + b;
    b := b*x + a[i]
    end;
val := b;  grad := c
end (* Horner *);
```

16.2 Solution of Polynomial Equations

There are old algebraic methods (similar to the quadratic formula but more complicated) for solving cubic and quartic equations. These methods are hardly ever used, and in any case it has been proved that no such formulae can exist for general polynomials of degree greater than 4. Instead, we compute real zeros numerically by Newton's method (see section 15.2):

$$x_{k+1} = x_k - p_n(x_k)/p_n'(x_k), \qquad k = 0,1,\dots$$

Newton's method comes into its own for polynomials. There is no difficulty over obtaining or evaluating the derivative; we can use Horner's scheme. Catastrophic divergence does not occur, although the sequence of iterates may still fail to converge (for example, there may be no real zeros), so we need to retain a cutoff on the number of iterations. There is the possibility that $p_n'(x_k)$ may be zero (see remarks at the end of section 15.3), and this should be guarded against. We also introduce an additional convergence test to stop the iteration if $p_n(x_k)$ is zero to machine accuracy.

Example 16.2

The following procedure may be more easily understood if it is compared with program Newton and procedure Secant in chapter 15. The *deflated polynomial* referred to in the procedure description will be discussed later.

```
procedure Polysol (n : degree;  var a : coeffs;  x, tol : real;
                   trace : boolean;  var b : coeffs;
                   var root : real;  var converged : boolean);
(* This procedure attempts to find a real root of the equation
           a[n]x^n + ... + a[1]x + a[0] = 0
   by Newton's method, using Horner's scheme to evaluate the poly-
   nomial and its derivative. The degree is supplied in parameter n
   of type degree = 0..maxdeg, where maxdeg is a positive integer
   constant. The coefficients a[0],...,a[n] are supplied in the
   array a of type coeffs = array[degree] of real. A starting value x
   and an absolute error tolerance tol must be supplied (tol may be
   set to 0.0 for full machine accuracy). If the procedure is called
   with trace set to true, intermediate iterates are written to the
   output file as a diagnostic aid.
   The computation terminates in one of two ways:
   (1) convergence is attained and the computed value is returned in
   root with converged set to true;
   (2) convergence is not attained after maxiter iterations - the
   latest value is returned in root with converged set to false.
   In case (1) the coefficients b[0],...,b[n-1] of the deflated
   polynomial are returned in the array b *)

   const
      maxiter  = 20;      (* maximum number of iterations allowed  *)
      rprec    = 5.0e-16; (* at least twice the relative precision *)
      smallreal = 1.0e-37; (* at least 10 times minimum real number *)

   var
      p, pd, correction : real;
      iter : integer;
      i    : degree;
```

```
<procedure Horner declared here>

begin    (* body of Polysol *)
iter := 0;  converged := false;
repeat
   Horner(n, a, x, p, pd);   (* evaluates polynomial p
                                 and derivative pd at x *)
   if abs(p) < smallreal then
      converged := true      (* p(x) is 'zero' *)
   else
      begin
      if abs(pd) > smallreal then
         begin  (* one step of Newton's method *)
         correction := -p/pd;
         x := x + correction;
         converged := (abs(correction)<tol) or
                      (abs(correction)<rprec*abs(x))
         end
      else
         (* derivative is 'zero', recover by
            shifting x an arbitrary amount *)
         x := x + 1.23;
      if trace then
         writeln('     ', x:20);
      iter := iter+1
      end
until converged or (iter = maxiter);

root := x;
if converged then
   begin  (* compute deflated polynomial *)
   b[n-1] := a[n];
   for i := n-2 downto 0 do
      b[i] := b[i+1]*root + a[i+1]
   end
end (* Polysol *);
```

The cubic $p_3(x) = x^3 - 12x + 7$ shown in figure 16.1 has three real zeros.

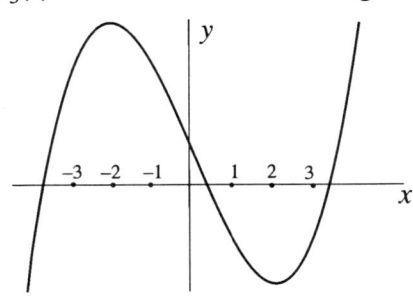

Figure 16.1 Graph of $y = x^3 - 12x + 7$

The following program can be used to find any of these zeros, given suitable starting values.

Example 16.3

```pascal
program TestPolysol (input, output);
(* This program illustrates the use of procedure Polysol to compute
   a real zero of a polynomial *)

const
   maxdeg = 10;      (* maximum degree of polynomial   *)
   tol    = 0.0;     (* full machine accuracy sought   *)
   trace  = true;    (* intermediate iterates required *)

type
   degree = 0..maxdeg;
   coeffs = array[degree] of real;

var
   i, n  : degree;
   a, b  : coeffs;
   root  : real;
   found : boolean;

<procedure Polysol declared here>

begin  (* main program *)
writeln('Real zero of a polynomial by Newton''s method ...');
writeln;
write('Enter degree n (1<=n<=', maxdeg:2, '):          '); readln(n);
write('Enter coefficients a[n]...a[0]:   ');
for i := n downto 0 do
   read(a[i]);
readln;
write('Enter initial approximation:     '); readln(root);
writeln;

Polysol(n, a, root, tol, trace, b, root, found); (* call procedure
                                                    to refine root *)
writeln;
if found then
   writeln('Computed zero = ', root:20)
else
   writeln('Newton''s method fails to converge');
writeln
end.
```

Test run:

We exercise the recovery path of Polysol by starting at $x_0 = 2$ where $p_3(x)$ has a turning point.

```
Real zero of a polynomial by Newton's method ...

Enter degree n (1<=n<=10):       3
Enter coefficients a[n]...a[0]:   1   0 -12   7
Enter initial approximation:      2.0
        3.2300000000000e+00
        3.12956489297211e+00
        3.1239999973008e+00
        3.1239831796592e+00
        3.1239831795058e+00
        3.1239831795058e+00
Computed zero =  3.1239831795058e+00
```

The Deflated Polynomial

Obtaining a zero α of $p_n(x)$ is equivalent to factorizing the polynomial as

$$p_n(x) = (x - \alpha)\, q_{n-1}(x)$$

where $q_{n-1}(x)$ is a polynomial of degree $n - 1$ called the *deflated polynomial*. According to equation (16.2), $q_{n-1}(x)$ is given by a final application of Horner's scheme to $p_n(x)$ (when $\bar{x} = \alpha$ and $b_{-1} \approx 0$). The coefficients $b_0, ..., b_{n-1}$ of the deflated polynomial are returned in the array parameter b of procedure Polysol.

Provided $n > 1$, we can seek a further zero of p_n by repeating the whole process to find a zero of the deflated polynomial q_{n-1}. However, this will be no more than an approximate zero of p_n, since α is necessarily inexact. The usual procedure is to take this approximate zero as a starting value and refine it by applying Newton's method to the original polynomial p_n. By repeated deflation, it is possible to obtain accurate values for all the real zeros of $p_n(x)$.

16.3 Order of Convergence

Example 16.4
The cubic equation

$$x^3 - 4x^2 + 5x - 2 = 0$$

has a *double root* at $x = 1$ and a *simple root* at $x = 2$ (equivalently, if we denote the polynomial by $p(x)$, then $p(1) = 0$, $p'(1) = 0$, $p''(1) \neq 0$ and $p(2) = 0$, $p'(2) \neq 0$).

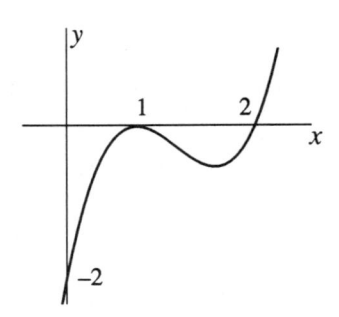

Figure 16.2   Graph of $y = x^3 - 4x^2 + 5x - 2$

We use program TestPolysol to compute the root $x = 1$ as accurately as possible.

Test run:

```
Real zero of a polynomial by Newton's method ...

Enter degree n (1<=n<=10):      3
Enter coefficients a[n]...a[0]:  1 -4  5 -2
Enter initial approximation:     0.0

        4.0000000000000e-01
        6.5263157894737e-01

        . . . . . . . . .
        . . . . . . . . .
        9.9998602306552e-01
        9.9999301147884e-01
        9.9999650571503e-01
        9.9999825281420e-01

Newton's method fails to converge
```

The output (20 iterations in all) is given in abbreviated form. It can be seen that the iterates are converging slowly to the double root at $x = 1$, but the cutoff operates before any convergence test is satisfied.

Newton's method for solving an equation $f(x) = 0$ suffers a serious loss of 'converging power' at a multiple root (i.e. where $f'(\alpha) = 0$). We can gain some insight into this by examining the *errors* $\varepsilon_k = 1.0 - x_k$ of the last four iterates above.

k	ε_k	$\varepsilon_k / \varepsilon_{k-1}$
17	14.0×10^{-6}	
18	7.0×10^{-6}	0.50
19	3.5×10^{-6}	0.50
20	1.75×10^{-6}	0.50

We see that the error decreases by an approximately constant factor (which happens to be 0.50 here) at each step. This type of convergence, slow and steady, is called *first order*.

Normally Newton's method goes much faster than this. It can be shown that, for a simple root (where $f'(\alpha) \neq 0$), the error at each step is approximately proportional to the *square* of the preceding error, i.e. $\varepsilon_k/\varepsilon_{k-1}^2 \to$ constant and $\varepsilon_k/\varepsilon_{k-1} \to 0$ as $k \to \infty$. This is called *second-order convergence*.

Further Developments

A polynomial of degree n has exactly n zeros, counting multiplicities and complex roots. The latter can be found by Newton's method as long as complex initial approximations are taken and complex arithmetic is used. An alternative often employed is *Bairstow's method*, which avoids complex arithmetic by extracting quadratic factors instead of linear factors as described in this chapter. Complex zeros can then be found by means of the formula for quadratic equations.

17. Systems of Linear Equations

One of the fundamental problems of numerical computation is to solve a *system of simultaneous linear equations*

$$a_{11}x_1 + a_{12}x_2 + \ldots + a_{1n}x_n = b_1$$
$$a_{21}x_1 + a_{22}x_2 + \ldots + a_{2n}x_n = b_2$$
$$\vdots$$
$$a_{n1}x_1 + a_{n2}x_2 + \ldots + a_{nn}x_n = b_n$$

where the coefficients $a_{11},\ldots, a_{nn}$ and the right hand sides $b_1,\ldots, b_n$ are known real numbers. The task is to find numerical values for the unknowns $x_1,\ldots, x_n$. Such systems often arise as a result of linearizing approximations made in harder problems, such as fitting a curve to a set of data points or solving differential equations subject to boundary conditions. It is therefore important to have efficient and accurate methods to deal with this problem.

17.1 Gaussian Elimination

Example 17.1
Solve the following system of linear equations by a method suitable for programming, with precautions against numerical error growth.

$$\begin{aligned}
4x_1 + 10x_2 + x_3 &= -5 \\
21x_1 + 3x_2 - 5x_3 &= 13 \\
x_1 + x_2 + 8x_3 &= 8
\end{aligned}$$

We shall employ a systematic elimination method. The general idea is to use the first equation to eliminate x_1 from equations 2, 3, ..., then use the (modified) second equation to eliminate x_2 from equations 3, ..., and so on. At the end of this process all the coefficients below the main diagonal will have been reduced to 0. This is known as *Gaussian elimination*.

First we reorder the equations so that the coefficient of largest absolute value in column 1 appears at the top (any solution of the system is unaffected by such reordering). Abstracting the coefficients, we obtain the table

$$\begin{array}{ccc|c} \boxed{21} & 3 & -5 & 13 \\ 4 & 10 & 1 & -5 \\ 1 & 1 & 8 & 8 \end{array}$$

The element $\underline{21}$ is called the *pivot* at this stage. Now we calculate the *multipliers*

$$m_{21} = 4/21 \approx 0.190$$
$$m_{31} = 1/21 \approx 0.048$$

(working to 3 decimal places). Subtracting m_{21} times row 1 from row 2, and m_{31} times row 1 from row 3 (not forgetting the right hand sides), we obtain the equivalent system

$$\begin{array}{ccc|c} 21 & 3 & -5 & 13 \\ 0 & \boxed{9.430} & 1.950 & -7.470 \\ 0 & 0.856 & 8.240 & 7.376 \end{array}$$

This is the end of the first elimination stage.

Next, the pivot is taken as $\underline{9.430}$, and we calculate the multiplier

$$m_{32} = 0.856/9.430 \approx 0.091$$

Subtracting m_{32} times row 2 from row 3, we obtain

$$\begin{array}{ccc|c} 21 & 3 & -5 & 13 \\ 0 & 9.430 & 1.950 & -7.470 \\ 0 & 0 & 8.063 & 8.056 \end{array}$$

This completes Gaussian elimination for the 3×3 case. The system is finally in *upper triangular form*, and the solution can be obtained by *back substitution*:

$$x_3 = 8.056/8.063 \approx 0.999$$
$$x_2 = (-7.470 - 1.950 \times 0.999)/9.430 \approx -0.999$$
$$x_1 = (13 - 3 \times (-0.999) + 5 \times 0.999)/21 \approx 1.000$$

Working with real numbers to finite precision, we have incurred rounding errors in the computation (the exact solution is $x_1 = 1$, $x_2 = -1$, $x_3 = 1$, as is easily checked). In larger systems the errors may grow and make the computed solution very inaccurate. A usually necessary precaution is *partial pivoting*: at each stage we inspect the elements in the pivotal column from the diagonal element downwards, find the largest in absolute value, and move this to the pivotal position by exchanging two whole equations. Then all the multipliers formed from this pivot will be ≤ 1 in absolute value. Algebraically this makes no difference to the solution, but in numerical computation this strategy acts to prevent the growth of rounding error. We performed partial pivoting at the first elimination stage in example 17.1 (see multipliers m_{21}, m_{31}); at the second stage the equations happened to be in the required order already (multiplier m_{32}).

Outline code for Gaussian elimination (without pivoting)

```
for k := 1 to n-1 do
   begin (* kth elimination stage *)
   pivot := A[k,k];
   for i := k+1 to n do
      begin (* work on row i>k *)
      mult := A[i,k]/pivot;
      for j := k+1 to n do
         A[i,j] := A[i,j] - mult*A[k,j];
         (* note that A[i,k] need not be set
            explicitly to 0 - this is assumed *)
      b[i] := b[i] - mult*b[k]
      end
   end
```

Figure 17.1:
Gaussian elimination

Outline code for back substitution

```
for i := n downto 1 do
   begin
   sum := b[i];
   for j := i+1 to n do
      sum := sum - A[i,j]*x[j];
   x[i] := sum/A[i,i]
   end
```

It should be understood that the system we have solved in example 17.1 can be expressed in matrix form as

$$\begin{bmatrix} 4 & 10 & 1 \\ 21 & 3 & -5 \\ 1 & 1 & 8 \end{bmatrix} \begin{bmatrix} x_1 \\ x_2 \\ x_3 \end{bmatrix} = \begin{bmatrix} -5 \\ 13 \\ 8 \end{bmatrix}$$

that is, $Ax = b$ for a certain 3×3 matrix A and vectors x and b. Now if A has an *inverse* (i.e. a matrix A^{-1} such that $A^{-1}A = I$ where I is the unit matrix), we could premultiply $Ax = b$ by A^{-1} to obtain the solution formally as $x = A^{-1}b$. There are various ways of computing the inverse if one exists. Unfortunately, these all require several times more work than solving any particular system $Ax = b$, so there are no short cuts.

An $n \times n$ system $Ax = b$ has a unique solution, which can be found numerically, if and only if the coefficient matrix A possesses an inverse. Otherwise, A is said to be *singular*. This will be indicated in the Gaussian elimination process by the appearance of a zero pivot (in practice, because of rounding error, a 'nearly zero' pivot), even with the strategy of partial pivoting. Singularity or near-singularity is an exceptional case, but one that we must consider if we wish to develop a robust program.

Ill-conditioned Systems

We recall from section 14.1 that a problem is said to be *ill-conditioned* if a small perturbation of the parameters or data can produce a large change in the solution. The condition of a linear system is determined by the coefficient matrix - specifically, by how close it is to singularity.

Consider the system of equations

$$4.0x + 5.8y = 9.8$$
$$2.0x + 3.0y = 5.0$$

Gaussian elimination yields the reduced system

$$4.0x + 5.8y = 9.8$$
$$0.1y = 0.1$$

with a coefficient 0.1 on the diagonal which, significantly, is much smaller than the preceding pivot 4.0. The exact solution is $x = 1.0$, $y = 1.0$.

If we change the coefficient 3.0 in the above system to 3.1, we obtain instead the reduced system

$$4.0x + 5.8y = 9.8$$
$$0.2y = 0.1$$

and the exact solution becomes $x = 1.725$, $y = 0.5$. If we now substitute the incorrect values $x = 1.725$, $y = 0.5$ back into the first system, we find that the equations are almost exactly satisfied. The *residuals* are

$$9.8 - 4.0 \times 1.725 - 5.8 \times 0.5 = 0.0$$
$$5.0 - 2.0 \times 1.725 - 3.0 \times 0.5 = 0.05$$

If we did not know any better, we might think that these values of x and y were a good approximation to a solution. In fact, the 'solution' is in error by 50–75%, but the residuals are at most 1% of the right hand side. This is typical of an ill-conditioned problem.

The rounding errors that inevitably arise in computing with real numbers can be regarded as pertubations of the data. If the problem is ill-conditioned, this means that the computed solution may be a poor approximation to the true solution. It is for this reason that precautions such as partial pivoting, and others to be mentioned later, are incorporated into programs for solving linear systems.

17.2 Application: Least Squares Polynomial

In section 11.3 we showed how to fit a polynomial of degree n

$$p_n(x) = a_0 + a_1x + \ldots + a_nx^n$$

to a set of data points (x_i, f_i), $i = 1, ..., m$ $(m > n)$ by least squares approximation. This leads to the *normal equations*, a system of $n + 1$ linear equations for the unknowns $a_0, a_1, ..., a_n$ (refer to procedure SetUp in example 11.4). We now show how to solve such a system by Gaussian elimination followed by back substitution. The task is simplified from a programming point of view by the fact that the normal equations are of a special type called *positive definite* for which partial pivoting is redundant (row exchanges would never be activated). However, for increasing values of n the normal equations become very ill-conditioned.

Example 17.2

```
program PolyFit (input, output);
(* This program fits a polynomial of degree n
          a[0] + a[1]x + ... + a[n]x^n
   to a set of data points (xi,fi) (not more than datamax) by least
   squares approximation. The degree n is restricted to 0<=n<=nmax.
   Input: degree n and a sequence of pairs x f, one pair on each line.
   Output: the coefficients a[0],...,a[n] and the root mean square
   deviation.
   NOTE: The program does not check that the xi are all distinct.
   If not more than n of these are distinct, any solution produced
   will be meaningless *)
const
   datamax   = 100;  (* maximum permitted number of data points   *)
   nmax      = 10;   (* maximum degree of approximating polynomial *)
   nmaxplus1 = 11;

type
   degree   = 0..nmax;
   datavec  = array[1..datamax] of real;
   coeffvec = array[degree] of real;
   coeffmat = array[degree, 0..nmaxplus1] of real;

var
   x, f : datavec;
   a    : coeffvec;
   C    : coeffmat;
   m    : integer;
   i, n : degree;

<procedure SetUp declared here
 - see example 11.4>
```

```
procedure Solve (n : degree;  var C : coeffmat;  var a : coeffvec);
(* Solves normal equations for least squares polynomial of degree n
   by Gaussian elimination and back substitution (pivoting is not
   required in this application). The coefficients of the normal
   equations are taken from columns 0..n of array C, the right hand
   side from column n+1. The solution is returned in vector a *)

   var
      i, k : degree;
      j    : integer;
      mult, pivot, sum : real;

   begin
   (* Gaussian elimination *)
   for k := 0 to n-1 do            (* note row/column 0 *)
      begin (* kth elimination stage *)
      pivot := C[k,k];
      for i := k+1 to n do
         begin
         mult := C[i,k]/pivot;
         for j := k+1 to n+1 do  (* note RHS column n+1 *)
            C[i,j] := C[i,j] - mult*C[k,j]
         end
      end;

   (* Back substitution *)
   for i := n downto 0 do
      begin
      sum := C[i,n+1];
      for j := i+1 to n do
         sum := sum - C[i,j]*a[j];
      a[i] := sum/C[i,i]
      end
   end (* Solve *);

function RMS (m : integer;  n : degree;
              var x, f : datavec; var a : coeffvec) : real;
(* Computes root mean square deviation of polynomial
        a[0] + a[1]x + ... + a[n]x^n
   from the data set (x[i],f[i]), i=1,...,m *)

   var
      sumsq, polval : real;
      i : integer;
      j : degree;

   begin
   sumsq := 0;
```

```
   for i := 1 to m do
      begin  (* evaluate polynomial at x[i] by Horner's scheme *)
      polval := a[n];
      for j := n-1 downto 0 do
         polval := polval*x[i] + a[j];
      sumsq := sumsq + sqr(polval-f[i])
      end;
   RMS := sqrt(sumsq/m)
   end (* RMS *);

begin         (* main program *)
readln(n);    (* value entered for n must lie in range 0..nmax *)
m := 0;       (* data counter *)
while not eof and (m < datamax) do
   begin  (* read data pair *)
   m := m+1;
   readln(x[m], f[m])
   end;
if not eof then
   writeln('ERROR: More than ', datamax:3, ' data points')
else
   begin
   writeln('Number of data points =', m:3);   writeln;
   if m<=n then  (* too few points for polynomial of degree n *)
      n := m-1;
   write('Least squares approximation by polynomial of degree ');
   writeln(n:2, ' ...'); writeln;
   SetUp(m, n, x, f, C);
   Solve(n, C, a);
   for i := 0 to n do   (* output solution *)
      writeln('    a[', i:1, '] = ', a[i]:10);
   writeln;
   writeln('RMS deviation = ', RMS(m, n, x, f, a):10)
   end
end.
```

Test runs:

The input is conveniently read from a data file.

```
   3
  -1.5     8.121
  -1.0     3.988
   0.0     1.007
   1.0     0.005
   1.5    -1.628
   2.0    -4.992
```

```
Number of data points =  6

Least squares approximation by polynomial of degree  3 ...
     a[0]  =   1.001e+00
     a[1]  =  -9.965e-01
     a[2]  =   9.988e-01
     a[3]  =  -9.998e-01

RMS deviation =  5.466e-03
```

The second test is with the same data set but degree 3 replaced by 5.

```
Number of data points =  6

Least squares approximation by polynomial of degree  5 ...
     a[0]  =   1.007e+00
     a[1]  =  -9.830e-01
     a[2]  =   9.848e-01
     a[3]  =  -1.009e+00
     a[4]  =   4.667e-03
     a[5]  =   8.762e-04

RMS deviation =  7.787e-15
```

[Fitting a polynomial of degree 5 to 6 data points is a case of interpolation, and the RMS deviation is theoretically zero. A small nonzero value is obtained because of rounding error from the finite precision of the computer, arising mainly in solving the 6×6 system of equations. The exact value is *machine dependent*.]

17.3 Solving Linear Systems

In this section we will develop a procedure for the general case of solving an $n \times n$ system of linear equations, $Ax = b$, by Gaussian elimination and back substitution with partial pivoting (see section 17.1). Some preliminary remarks are in order.

In solving such systems for fairly large values of n, most of the computational effort goes into the elimination part and much less into back substitution (analysis shows approximately $2n^3/3$ arithmetic operations compared with n^2). It frequently happens that we wish to solve systems with the same coefficient matrix A but different right hand sides b. Since most of the work is done once and for all in elimination (i.e. reducing the matrix A to upper triangular form), is there any way we can save the results of elimination and use these repeatedly?

This can be accomplished as follows. The multipliers $m_{ik} = a_{ik}/a_{kk}$ for $i > k$ (see figure 17.1) can be associated in a natural way with a *lower triangular* matrix

$$\begin{bmatrix} \cdot & & & & & \\ m_{21} & \cdot & & & & \\ m_{31} & m_{32} & \cdot & & & \\ \cdot & \cdot & & \cdot & & \\ \cdot & \cdot & & & \cdot & \\ \cdot & \cdot & & & & \cdot \\ m_{n1} & m_{n2} & \cdot & \cdot & \cdot & \cdot & \cdot & \cdot \end{bmatrix}$$

In our procedure we will *overwrite* each array element A[i,k] (which theoretically becomes zero) with the corresponding multiplier m_{ik}. The same array can hold the reduced upper triangular form. Then for any given coefficient matrix, Gaussian elimination need only be performed once; the multipliers and upper triangle saved in the array A can be used for any number of different right hand sides (see Exercise Set D).

In implementing partial pivoting we shall not interchange equations explicitly. A record of the row indices will be kept in a vector row, initially in the order $1,...,n$, and instead of interchanging actual equations we interchange the corresponding components of the vector row. The element in the (i,j)th position of array A is then referenced as A[row[i],j] instead of A[i,j], and similarly for the right hand side. Apart from efficiency, the motivation for this is the same as before: if we wish to deal with different right hand sides, we must keep a record of the row permutations resulting from partial pivoting, and this technique of *indirect addressing* is the simplest way.

How shall we detect if the coefficient matrix is singular? Mathematically this means that the system has no solution, or at least no unique solution, and this will be signalled by the appearance of a zero pivot even with the strategy of partial pivoting. Back substitution would then be impossible ($a_{ii} = 0$ for some i). In practice, because of rounding error, a pivot with the exact value zero is very unlikely to arise. Our test for a 'zero' pivot at the kth elimination stage is therefore

$$\max_{k \leq i \leq n} |a_{ik}| < \varepsilon$$

where ε is a roundoff threshold which (for simplicity) we take to be a constant, at least 10 times the relative precision of the computer. If at any stage a pivot greater than ε cannot be found, we shall consider that the matrix is singular to within the roundoff error level and any solution that might be computed would be meaningless; in that case the computation will be abandoned with a boolean parameter set to indicate singularity.

The following constant and type definitions are used.

```
nmax      = ...;    (* maximum permitted order of linear system *)
order     = 1..nmax;
rvector   = array[order] of real;
ivector   = array[order] of integer;
matrix    = array[order,order] of real;
```

Example 17.3

```
procedure LinSolve (n : order;  var A : matrix;  var x, b : rvector;
                    var row : ivector;  var singular : boolean);
(* This procedure solves an nxn system of linear equations Ax = b by
   Gaussian elimination and back substitution. Array A is overwritten
   with the reduced upper triangular form and the multipliers.
   Partial pivoting is implemented by indirect addressing; vector row
   returns the permuted row indices. If at any stage a pivot cannot be
   found greater than the constant eps, the matrix is considered to be
   singular to within the roundoff error level and the computation
   is abandoned with the parameter singular set to true. Otherwise
   the computed solution is returned in vector x *)

const
   eps = 2.5e-15;   (* machine-dependent constant, at least
                       10 times the relative precision *)
var
   size, maxsize, pivot, mult, sum : real;
   i, k, isave, pivotrow, rowi  : order;
   j : integer;

begin
singular := false; (* switched to true if A is
                      found to be singular *)
for i := 1 to n do
   row[i] := i;     (* initialize row indices *)

(* Gaussian elimination *)
k := 1;
while (k < n) and not singular do  (* kth elimination stage  *)
   begin                           (* seek pivot in column k *)
   maxsize := 0;
   for i := k to n do
      begin
      size := abs(A[row[i],k]);
      if size > maxsize then
         begin
         maxsize := size;  isave :=i
         end
      end;
```

```
      if maxsize < eps then
         singular := true  (* pivotal sub-column all zero
                                   to within rounding error *)
      else
         begin   (* a pivot has been found *)
         pivotrow := row[isave];  pivot := A[pivotrow, k];
         (* exchange indices of rows isave and k *)
         row[isave] := row[k];  row[k] := pivotrow;
         (* elimination using pivot *)
         for i := k+1 to n do
            begin
            rowi := row[i];
            mult := A[rowi,k]/pivot;
            for j := k+1 to n do
               A[rowi,j] := A[rowi,j] - mult*A[pivotrow,j];
            b[rowi] := b[rowi] - mult*b[pivotrow];
            A[rowi,k] := mult   (* save multiplier *)
            end
         end;
      k := k+1
      end (* kth elimination stage *);
   if abs(A[row[n],n]) < eps then
      singular := true;

   if not singular then    (* back substitution *)
      for i := n downto 1 do
         begin
         rowi := row[i];  sum := b[rowi];
         for j := i+1 to n do
            sum := sum - A[rowi,j]*x[j];
         x[i] := sum/A[rowi,i]
         end
   end (* LinSolve *);
```

In this procedure we have tacitly assumed that the coefficients of the equations do not vary greatly in magnitude. If this is not the case, some form of *scaling* is necessary. Indeed, we could force any selection of pivots by a suitable pre-scaling of the rows of the coefficient matrix, and we must decide on some standardization to justify the partial pivoting strategy. A common method is *row equilibration*: each equation is multiplied through by a factor so that the largest coefficient in absolute value is equal to 1. In a computer program we would not multiply the equations explicitly; instead the scale factors would be stored in a vector and used only in the process of selecting pivots. This avoids introducing superfluous rounding errors by multiplying the matrix elements, and also leaves the right hand side unaffected.

Triangular Factorization

We return to the 3×3 problem of example 17.1 and arrange to save the results of elimination. Working to 3 decimal places, the multipliers were found to be $m_{21} = 0.190$, $m_{31} = 0.048$, $m_{32} = 0.091$. These can be placed in a *unit lower triangular matrix*

$$\mathbf{L} = \begin{bmatrix} 1 & 0 & 0 \\ 0.190 & 1 & 0 \\ 0.048 & 0.091 & 1 \end{bmatrix}$$

The reduced upper triangular form was found to be

$$\mathbf{U} = \begin{bmatrix} 21 & 3 & -5 \\ 0 & 9.430 & 1.950 \\ 0 & 0 & 8.063 \end{bmatrix}$$

It is straightforward to verify by matrix multiplication that

$$\mathbf{LU} = \begin{bmatrix} 21 & 3 & -5 \\ 3.990 & 10 & 1 \\ 1.008 & 1.002 & 8.000 \end{bmatrix}$$

Allowing for rounding error, this is the same as the original coefficient matrix $\mathbf{A}$ of example 17.1, with rows 1 and 2 interchanged.

As this example suggests, Gaussian elimination applied to a system $\mathbf{Ax} = \mathbf{b}$ yields the *triangular factorization* $\mathbf{A} = \mathbf{LU}$, with account taken of row exchanges in pivoting. The system $\mathbf{Ax} = \mathbf{b}$ can then be written as $\mathbf{LUx} = \mathbf{b}$ and decomposed into two 'triangular' systems

$$\mathbf{Ly} = \mathbf{b}$$
$$\mathbf{Ux} = \mathbf{y}$$

The first system can be solved for $\mathbf{y}$ by *forward* substitution, then the second for $\mathbf{x}$ by *back* substitution. The resulting vector $\mathbf{x}$ is the solution of the original problem.

Gaussian elimination is one way of obtaining triangular factors of a matrix $\mathbf{A}$. Another way is to determine the elements of the matrices $\mathbf{L}$ and $\mathbf{U}$ so that, when they are multiplied together, $\mathbf{LU} = \mathbf{A}$. The direct calculation of $\mathbf{L}$ and $\mathbf{U}$ in this way, followed by the solution of $\mathbf{Ly} = \mathbf{b}$ and $\mathbf{Ux} = \mathbf{y}$, is called *Doolittle's method* (*Crout's method* is a variant in which $\mathbf{U}$ instead of $\mathbf{L}$ is chosen to have unit diagonal elements). Doolittle's method is equivalent to Gaussian elimination; the same factors are obtained, the same amount of arithmetic is performed, and the error behaviour is the same. These factorization methods can be convenient on hand calculators, for which they were designed; for automatic computation in the case of general linear systems they have no significant advantage over Gaussian elimination.

17.4 Iterative Methods

The approach we have considered so far for solving linear systems is called *direct*; the solution is obtained after a fixed number of steps which can be calculated in advance. This is possible only because linear systems are particularly simple. There are also methods which, like most in numerical computation, are *iterative*, involving a theoretically infinite process of successive approximation. In some special applications this may be preferable to a direct approach.

To derive an iterative method, we write the system as though each equation had been solved for one of the unknowns:

$$x_i = (b_i - \sum_{j=1}^{i-1} a_{ij}x_j - \sum_{j=i+1}^{n} a_{ij}x_j)/a_{ii}, \quad i = 1, \dots, n$$

Provided no $a_{ii} = 0$, this can form the basis of an iteration. Of course, the quantities $x_1, \dots, x_{i-1}$ and $x_{i+1}, \dots, x_n$ required on the right hand side are unknown. There are two variants, depending on the values substituted for these unknowns.

Jacobi method

$$x_i^{(k+1)} = (b_i - \sum_{\substack{j=1 \\ j \neq i}}^{n} a_{ij}x_j^{(k)})/a_{ii}$$

Gauss-Seidel method

$$x_i^{(k+1)} = (b_i - \sum_{j=1}^{i-1} a_{ij}x_j^{(k+1)} - \sum_{j=i+1}^{n} a_{ij}x_j^{(k)})/a_{ii}$$

where in each case k denotes the iteration number, starting at 0 and continuing as far as desired. As initial values we might take each $x_i^{(0)} = 0$ if no better estimate is available.

The distinction between the two methods is that in the Jacobi method the old set of values for the components is used on the right hand side until the end of a complete cycle ($i = 1, \dots, n$) when the $x_i^{(k)}$ are all updated simultaneously, whereas in the Gauss-Seidel method a new value for each component is used as soon as it has been calculated. This makes the latter slightly easier to program. One iteration of the Gauss-Seidel method might be expressed as

```
for i := 1 to n do
   begin  (* calculate new value for x[i] *)
   sum := b[i];
   for j := 1 to n do
      sum := sum - A[i,j]*x[j];
   x[i] := x[i] + sum/A[i,i]
   end
```

This fragment, in which an $n \times n$ array A appears, is for illustration only. The purpose of employing iterative methods is precisely to avoid having an $n \times n$ array to store the coefficients. Iterative methods are used for solving *large*, *sparse systems*, e.g. thousands of equations with only a few nonzero coefficients in each row, which arise in special applications (finite difference methods for certain partial differential equations). The question of convergence must then be investigated, and the rate of convergence accelerated. Iterative methods should not be used for solving the systems of linear equations that you ordinarily meet.

Further Developments

The direct methods we have described in this chapter are satisfactory for solving non-sparse systems of linear equations, certainly up to orders of several hundred. In general, Gaussian elimination with scaling and partial pivoting, or equivalent factorization methods, are the appropriate choice. If the coefficient matrix has the properties of *symmetry* and *positive definiteness*, which may be inferred on theoretical or physical grounds, then the special factorization method known as *Cholesky decomposition* is more efficient.

In some important applications large coefficient matrices arise with all the nonzero elements clustered about the main diagonal (*tridiagonal* or more general *band systems* - see section 18.4). Direct methods, modified to take account of the special structure, can be used to solve these systems efficiently up to a very high order. Large, sparse systems which do not exhibit band structure are a more difficult problem. If the nonzero elements consist of predictable values occurring in a regular pattern, which can be computed when required and therefore need not be stored, one can attempt to solve such systems by iteration using *successive overrelaxation* or *conjugate gradient* methods. Otherwise, specialized algorithms are required which use techniques from the fields of graph theory and data structures; this is an active area of research.

It should be pointed out that much numerical computation in practice is carried out using *mathematical software libraries*. A library is a collection of subprograms, written to the highest current standards, for undertaking well-defined computations such as solving a general (or positive definite or band) system of linear equations. The user writes a program to call a library routine and provides it with specified inputs (a library mechanism is an extension to standard Pascal but is available in some form in virtually all implementations). It is not necessary to understand in detail how such library routines work, but in order to use them sensibly it is desirable to know something of the concepts and terminology of numerical analysis. Two of the most widely used numerical software libraries, intended mainly for FORTRAN programmers, are LINPACK (for solving linear algebraic systems) and NAG (which covers the whole range of numerical computation). Further details and references will be found in the text by Gerald and Wheatley listed in the Further Reading section at the end of this book.

18. Differential Equations

Example 18.1

The bacteria cultured in a Petri dish have a population $p(t)$ which is a function of elapsed time in days. The main factor governing the rate of growth of population is a term directly proportional to p. However, there are also terms representing negative effects (even bugs suffer from overcrowding); in a simple model these terms may be taken proportional to p^2. Thus the differential equation for $p(t)$ is

$$dp/dt = ap - bp^2$$

where a, b are positive constants and $p(0)$ is known. This is said to be an *initial value problem*. The equation is an *ordinary differential equation* (ODE) because no partial derivatives are involved, and *first order* since only the first derivative of the dependent variable p occurs.

What is the population $p(t)$ after 2, 5, 10 days? The variables can be separated and the equation integrated by a substitution, but not trivially; further correction terms would make it impossible to solve analytically. In fact most differential equations which arise in practice are of intractable type. In this chapter we will develop some of the numerical methods that can be used to solve commonly occurring differential equations.

18.1 Euler's Method

We consider the initial value problem in the standard form

$$y'(x) = f(x,y), \qquad y(x_0) = y_0 \tag{18.1}$$

where f is a given function called the *derivative function*, and the condition $y(x_0) = y_0$ is the *initial condition* (in example 18.1 which of the variables correspond to x and y, and what is f ?). Under fairly general conditions studied in the theory of differential equations, there exists a unique solution $y(x)$ to (18.1) over a range $x_0 \leq x < X$ (where X may be ∞). Our problem is to find $y(x)$, either as a formula or as a table of numerical values.

In a numerical approach we choose a set of discrete points x_1, x_2, ... and seek to calculate approximations Y_1, Y_2, ... to $y(x_1)$, $y(x_2)$, ... (Once such a numerical solution has been obtained, approximate values at non-tabulated points can be found, if desired, by the interpolation methods of chapter 12.) The basic problem can be stated simply as follows: given $Y_i \approx y(x_i)$, compute $Y_{i+1} \approx y(x_{i+1})$, starting with $i = 0$ where the exact value $y(x_0)$ is known.

The oldest and simplest way of doing this is to replace $y'(x)$ at $x = x_i$, $y = Y_i$ by $(Y_{i+1} - Y_i)/h$, where $h = x_{i+1} - x_i$ (see figure 18.1). Substituting into equation (18.1), we immediately obtain

$$Y_{i+1} = Y_i + hf(x_i, Y_i), \quad i = 0, 1, 2, ...$$

which, with $Y_0 = y_0$, is a recurrence relation defining the approximations Y_1, Y_2, ... This is *Euler's method*.

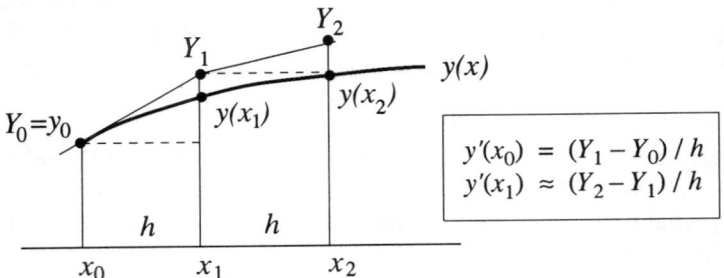

$$y'(x_0) = (Y_1 - Y_0)/h$$
$$y'(x_1) \approx (Y_2 - Y_1)/h$$

Figure 18.1   The first two steps of Euler's method   ($i = 0, 1$)

The Modified Euler Method

Although Euler's method is easy to program using a **for** loop, it provides only a low-order approximation requiring a small step size h for tolerable accuracy (and the more steps we have to perform, the more work). An improved version can be developed as follows.

First calculate $k_1 = hf(x_i, Y_i)$. This is Euler's estimate of the increase in the y value from x_i to $x_i + h$. Next calculate a similar estimate but taking the (approximate) gradient at the right hand end of the step: $k_2 = hf(x_i + h, Y_i + k_1)$. Note that k_1 and k_2 are both estimates of the increase in y over the *same step*. Finally take the average

$$Y_{i+1} = Y_i + (k_1 + k_2)/2, \quad i = 0, 1, 2, ... \qquad (18.2)$$

This is the *modified Euler method*. It also is easy to program; we give a Pascal function to compute one step, $x \rightarrow x + h$.

```
function ModEuler (function f(x,y:real) : real;
                   x, h, y : real) : real;
(* Given the value of y at x, dy/dx = f(x,y) and step size h,
   this function returns an approximation to y(x+h) by the
   modified Euler method *)

   var
       k : real;

   begin
   k := h*f(x,y);
   ModEuler := y + 0.5*(k + h*f(x+h, y+k))
   end (* ModEuler *);
```

The error of the computed value Y_i at any point x_i, $E(x_i) = y(x_i) - Y_i$, is called the *global error*. It can be shown that for well-behaved problems, the global error of the modified Euler method is asymptotically proportional to h^2; for any *fixed* point x, $E(x)/h^2$ tends to a constant as $h \to 0$. Thus, if we halve h and perform twice as many steps to reach x, the error $E(x)$ decreases in the limit by a factor of $2^2 = 4$. Just as in numerical integration, we can use this to extrapolate. Let $Y_i[h]$ and $Y_{2i}[h/2]$ denote the respective approximations to $y(x)$, then, as in equation (13.2),

$$E(x) \approx (Y_{2i}[h/2] - Y_i[h])/3$$

and an improved approximation is given by

$$y(x) = Y_{2i}[h/2] + E(x)$$

Application to Example 18.1

```
program Population (output);
(* This program calculates approximations p(1),...,p(lastday)
   to p(t) subject to the growth equation given in function PopGro
   below. The differential equation is solved by two parallel
   applications of the modified Euler method with step sizes 1.0
   and 0.5. Error bounds are estimated by extrapolation *)
const
   lastday = 10;
   start   = 10000;  (* initial population *)

var
   p, q, t, errest : real;
   day : 1..lastday;
```

```
function PopGro (t, p : real) : real;
(* Derivative function for dp/dt. Note that two real parameters
   are required to conform with f(x,y) in function ModEuler *)

   const
      a = 0.5;
      b = 1.0e-5;

   begin
   PopGro := (a-b*p)*p
   end;

<function ModEuler declared here>

begin   (* main program *)
p := start;  q := start;  (* initialize two parallel approximations *)
writeln;
writeln('     DAY     POPULATION    ERROR BOUND');
writeln;
for day := 1 to lastday do
   begin
   t := day-1;
   p := ModEuler(PopGro, t, 1.0, p);
   q := ModEuler(PopGro, t, 0.5, q);        (* first  half step *)
   q := ModEuler(PopGro, t+0.5, 0.5, q);    (* second half step *)
   errest := (q-p)/3;      (* error estimate by extrapolation *)
   writeln(day:8, round(q+errest):12, round(abs(errest)):12)
   end;
writeln
end.
```

Test run:

DAY	POPULATION	ERROR BOUND
1	14590	18
2	20224	36
3	26412	52
4	32433	66
5	37639	78
6	41699	84
7	44619	83
8	46597	75
9	47883	63
10	48697	50

18.2 Runge-Kutta Methods

The modified Euler method defined by equation (18.2) is one example of the so-called *Runge-Kutta methods* in which estimates of the gradient are calculated at suitably chosen points in the interval $[x_i, x_i + h]$ and used to generate the increment of the Y value. A more powerful method of this type is the classical *Runge-Kutta 4 method* (RK4), which works as follows.

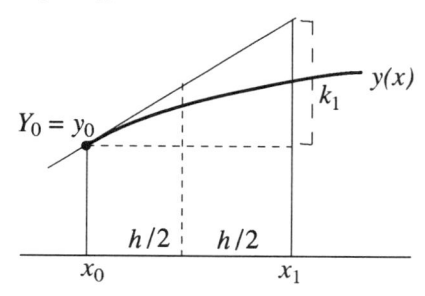

Figure 18.2   The first step of RK4 (i = 0)

First calculate $k_1 = hf(x_i, Y_i)$, as in Euler's method. Next calculate

$$k_2 = hf(x_i + h/2, Y_i + k_1/2)$$
$$k_3 = hf(x_i + h/2, Y_i + k_2/2)$$

(these are both estimates of the increase in y over a *full step*, i.e. k_2 and k_3 are comparable to k_1). Finally calculate a fourth estimate $k_4 = hf(x_i + h, Y_i + k_3)$, and take a weighted mean

$$Y_{i+1} = Y_i + (k_1 + 2k_2 + 2k_3 + k_4)/6, \quad i = 0, 1, 2, \ldots$$

This is not much more difficult to program than the modified Euler method.

Example 18.2

```
function RK4 (function f(x,y:real) : real;
                          x, h, y : real) : real;
(* Given the value of y at x, dy/dx = f(x,y) and step size h,
   this function returns an approximation to y(x+h) by the
   Runge-Kutta 4 method *)

var
    k, sum : real;
    i      : 1..2;

begin
k := h*f(x,y);   sum := k;
```

```
for i := 1 to 2 do
   begin
   k := h*f(x+h/2, y+k/2);
   sum := sum + 2*k
   end;
RK4 := y + (sum + h*f(x+h, y+k))/6
end (* RK4 *);
```

Four evaluations of the derivative function f are required per step, but as RK4 is normally much more accurate than the preceding methods a larger step size can be employed.

18.3 Systems and Higher-order Equations

Suppose we have n dependent variables, $y_1(x), \ldots, y_n(x)$, and a system of n simultaneous first-order differential equations with initial conditions all given at the same point:

$$dy_1/dx = f_1(x, y_1, \ldots, y_n), \qquad y_1(x_0) = y_{0,1}$$
$$\vdots \qquad \qquad \vdots \qquad\qquad\qquad \vdots \qquad\quad \vdots$$
$$dy_n/dx = f_n(x, y_1, \ldots, y_n), \qquad y_n(x_0) = y_{0,n}$$

This is conveniently summarized in vector notation as

$$\mathbf{y}' = \mathbf{f}(x, \mathbf{y}), \qquad \mathbf{y}(x_0) = \mathbf{y}_0 \tag{18.3}$$

Such a system can be solved by any of the methods we have described for single equations. It should be understood that there is still only one *independent* variable x, and we consider one step $x \rightarrow x + h$ as before.

The modified Euler method could be applied to (18.3) as follows (it is instructive to work through this in terms of components for the cases $n = 1, 2$, comparing with equation (18.2)).

(1) Compute the vectors

$$\mathbf{k} = h\mathbf{f}(x, \mathbf{y}), \quad \textit{ytemp} = \mathbf{y} + \mathbf{k}$$

(2) Take the vector

$$\mathbf{y} + 0.5\,(\mathbf{k} + h\mathbf{f}(x + h, \textit{ytemp}))$$

as an approximation to $\mathbf{y}(x + h)$.

We implement this as a Pascal procedure. The vectors y, ytemp and k are of type

```
vector = array[range] of real
```

where

```
range = 1..n
```

```
procedure SystemStep(function f(x:real; var y:vector; i:range) : real;
                        n : integer;  x, h : real;  var y : vector);
(* Given the vector y at x, dy[i]/dx = f(x,y,i) for i = 1,...,n, and
   step h, this procedure returns an approximation to the vector y
   at x+h by the modified Euler method *)

   var
      k, ytemp : vector;
      i        : range;

   begin
   for i := 1 to n do
      begin
      k[i] := h*f(x,y,i);  ytemp[i] := y[i]+k[i]
      end;
   for i := 1 to n do
      y[i] := y[i] + 0.5*(k[i] + h*f(x+h, ytemp, i))
   end (* SystemStep *);
```

Higher-order Equations

So far we have outlined various methods for solving first-order differential equations (and in fact there are other approaches that have not been mentioned). At this point one would be justified in asking: what about higher-order equations? After all, many of the differential equations of applied mathematics and science are second order. Fortunately, in the case of initial value problems, exactly the same methods can be used.

Consider a second-order equation

$$y'' = g(x, y, y')$$

with initial conditions $y(x_0) = y_0$, $y'(x_0) = \gamma_0$ (both given at the same point x_0). This is of a type that arises frequently in mechanics and many other areas. We can transform it into a pair of first-order equations by introducing a new dependent variable $z(x) = y'(x)$. The result is a system

$$y' = z(x), \qquad y(x_0) = y_0$$
$$z' = g(x, y, z), \qquad z(x_0) = \gamma_0$$

which is a special case of (18.3).

A similar transformation can be applied to initial value problems of any order provided they are *explicit*, that is, if it is possible to isolate the highest derivative on one side of the equation. For an nth order equation the result is a system of n simultaneous first-order equations, which can be solved by the methods already described.

Example 18.3

A light mortar shell is fired by accident vertically upwards. The height $s(t)$ satisfies the differential equation

$$\ddot{s} = -g - \dot{s}(a + b|\dot{s}|)$$

(note that the 'drag' terms have the correct sign, always opposing the motion provided the constants a and b are positive). How much time have the gun crew to get out of the way? Output a table of the height and velocity of the shell throughout its flight, given an initial velocity of 110 metres/sec and the values of the constants in MKS units:

$$g = 9.81, \quad a = 7.66 \times 10^{-3}, \quad b = 6.91 \times 10^{-5}$$

This problem can be solved as a system of two first-order equations,

$$
\begin{aligned}
ds/dt &= v, & s(0) &= 0 \\
dv/dt &= -g - v(a + b|v|), & v(0) &= 110
\end{aligned}
$$

The correspondence with the general case (18.3) is given by

$$
\begin{array}{ccc}
t & s & v \\
x & y_1 & y_2 & (n = 2)
\end{array}
$$

```
program ShellShock (output);
(* This program outputs a table of the height and velocity, at
   intervals of timestep seconds, of a projectile shot vertically
   upwards subject to the equation of motion
          dv/dt = -g - v*(a + b*abs(v))
   See function f below for the constants a and b. The differential
   equation is solved, together with ds/dt = v, by the modified
   Euler method for a system of n equations *)
const
   n        = 2;
   timestep = 1.0;
   vinit    = 110.0;  (* initial velocity *)

type
   range  = 1..n;
   vector = array[range] of real;

var
   t : real;     (* elapsed time *)
   y : vector;   (* y[1] = s, y[2] = v *)
```

```
function f (t : real;  var y : vector;  i : range) : real;
(* Derivative function for dy[i]/dt *)

   const
      a = 7.66e-3;  b = 6.91e-5;
      g = 9.81;

   begin
   case i of
      1:  f := y[2];    (* ds/dt = v *)
      2:  f := -g - y[2]*(a + b*abs(y[2]))  (* dv/dt = ....
                                       see program header *)

      end
   end (* f *);

<procedure SystemStep declared here>

begin  (* main program *)
(* Initialization *)
t := 0;  y[1] := 0;  y[2] := vinit;
writeln;
writeln(' TIME (secs)    HEIGHT (metres)    VELOCITY (metres/sec)');
writeln;
repeat
   writeln(t:7:1, round(y[1]):17, y[2]:19:1);
   SystemStep(f, n, t, timestep, y);
   t := t + timestep
until y[1] <= 0;
writeln(t:7:1, round(y[1]):17, '                 BOOM!')
end.
```

Test run:

TIME (secs)	HEIGHT (metres)	VELOCITY (metres/sec)
0.0	0	110.0
1.0	104	98.6
2.0	197	87.5
3.0	279	76.6
4.0	350	65.9
5.0	411	55.4
6.0	461	45.0
7.0	501	34.8
8.0	531	24.7
9.0	550	14.7
10.0	560	4.8
11.0	560	-5.0
12.0	550	-14.7

13.0	531	-24.4
14.0	501	-33.9
15.0	463	-43.3
16.0	415	-52.6
17.0	358	-61.7
18.0	291	-70.7
19.0	216	-79.6
20.0	132	-88.3
21.0	40	-96.8
22.0	-61	BOOM!

18.4   Boundary Value Problems

If the conditions necessary to fix the solution of a differential equation are given at more than one point, the problem is said to be a *boundary value problem*. For example, with a second-order ODE one might be given $y(a) = \alpha$ and $y(b) = \beta$ where $a < b$, and have to determine $y(x)$ for $a < x < b$. We could choose a step size of $h = (b - a)/n$ and attempt to compute approximations $Y_i \approx y(a + ih)$, $1 \leq i \leq n{-}1$. However, boundary value problems are not directly amenable to the step-by-step methods we have used so far, because there is not enough information to start the process at any single point.

The alternative is to incorporate the boundary values and solve the problem at all points simultaneously. To do this we can replace the derivatives at each of the points $x_i = a + ih$ by finite-difference approximations, of which the simplest are

$$y'(x_i) = (Y_{i+1} - Y_{i-1})/2h \qquad (18.4)$$
$$y''(x_i) = (Y_{i+1} - 2Y_i + Y_{i-1})/h^2 \qquad (18.5)$$

(these equations are obtained from formulae (14.3) and (14.4) of chapter 14 by dropping the $O(h^2)$ error term and replacing the true values $y(x_i)$ by approximations Y_i).

A further complication is that the boundary conditions may also involve derivatives. If the differential equation and the boundary conditions are *linear* (*y* and any of its derivatives appearing only as linear combinations), then the result of the *discretization* process above is a system of simultaneous linear equations which can be solved for the unknowns Y_i.

Example 18.4
A problem of particle motion in quantum mechanics gives rise to the differential equation

$$y''(x) = x\,y(x) + x^2$$

where the 'wave function' $y(x)$ is defined for all $x \geq 0$. It is known that $y(0) = 1$ and $y'(1) = 0$; the problem is to find the value $y(1)$.

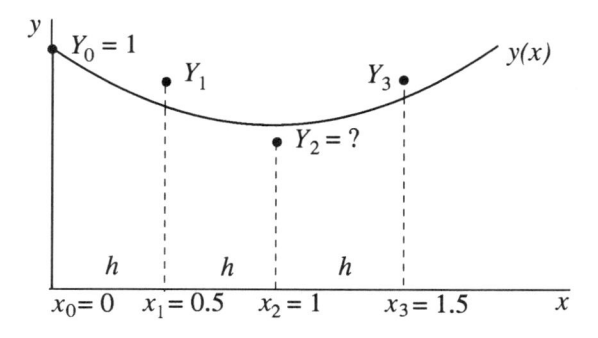

Figure 18.3 Boundary value problem with h = 1/2

We choose a step size $h = 1/2$ and make the replacement (18.5) in the differential equation at $x_1 = 0.5$ and $x_2 = 1$. The results are

$$(Y_2 - 2Y_1 + Y_0) / (1/2)^2 = 0.5 Y_1 + 0.5^2$$
$$(Y_3 - 2Y_2 + Y_1) / (1/2)^2 = 1.0 Y_2 + 1.0^2$$

The reason for extending the points to x_3 in figure 18.3 is that the boundary condition at x_2 involves a derivative, $y'(x_2) = 0$, and we need Y_3 in this case to make the replacement (18.4) :

$$(Y_3 - Y_1)/(2 \times 1/2) = 0$$

Together with $Y_0 = 1$, these equations simplify to a pair

$$34 \, Y_1 - 16 \, Y_2 = 15$$
$$8 \, Y_1 - 9 \, Y_2 = 1$$

from which we easily find

$$Y_2 = 0.48 \quad (\approx y(1))$$

Naturally this is a rather crude approximation. Higher accuracy can be obtained if we take a smaller step size $h = 1/n$. The resulting system of n linear equations is of a special form called *tridiagonal* (the elements of the coefficient matrix are zero outside a band of three diagonals). Such systems can be solved very efficiently by elimination. Carrying this out for $n = 20$ and $n = 40$ (with the aid of the computer!), we obtain respectively

$$y(1) \approx 0.54693, \qquad y(1) \approx 0.54745$$

It can be shown that the discretization method we have employed for this problem has an error proportional to h^2 as $h \to 0$. Using the by now familiar extrapolation technique, we estimate the error as

$$(0.54745 - 0.54693)/3 = 0.00017$$

and finally calculate

$$y(1) \approx 0.54745 + 0.00017$$
$$= 0.5476 \quad \text{correct to at least 3 decimal places}$$

Further Developments

The intention in this chapter has been no more than to give a flavour of the numerical methods that can be used to solve ordinary differential equations. This is an active area of research, and anyone who needs to make serious use of such methods should consult a more specialized work. For an overview and references one might start with the relevant chapters of the text by Burden and Faires listed in the Further Reading section at the end of this book.

   One of the difficulties that can arise with recurrence relations, which underlie most numerical methods for initial value problems, is *numerical instability*. It is usual to consider the test problem $y' = -\lambda y$, with solution of the form $y = Ae^{-\lambda x}$ $(\lambda > 0)$, and investigate whether a numerical method can reproduce the decreasing exponential solution. In most cases it is found that there is a critical value $\bar{h}$ such that, for $h > \bar{h}/\lambda$, the numerical solution Y is not merely inaccurate but completely wrong (i.e. $|Y|$ increases with x instead of decreasing). This imposes an unavoidable constraint on the usable step size. For single equations using Runge-Kutta 4 or even the modified Euler method this restriction is normally not very burdensome; for systems of equations, however, the situation can be quite different.

   In a variety of applications, problems arise involving processes with significantly different time scales (we are now thinking of the variable x as 'time'). The general solution $y(x)$ might then consist of steady-state terms together with rapidly decaying transients such as $e^{-\lambda x}$ with λ large and positive. Although the latter contribute almost nothing to the value of $y(x)$, in many cases we would be forced to use a very small step size to avoid numerical instability. Systems of differential equations exhibiting this difficult behaviour are called *stiff*.

   There are also *multistep* methods for solving differential equations, in which information from several previous steps is used; in the standard *implicit* form a nonlinear equation or nonlinear system is solved to compute each new approximation. For some problems, notably stiff systems, these methods have advantages over the one-step methods we have been considering.

Exercise Set D

15.1 Write a program to implement the iterative scheme
$$x_{k+1} = x_k(2 - cx_k), \qquad k = 0,1, \ldots$$
$(c \neq 0)$, with a suitable convergence test and cutoff. What will this iteration compute if it converges, i.e. what is the value of α such that $x_k \to \alpha$ as $k \to \infty$? Test your ideas by experimenting with the program. Having decided what it computes, establish the formula as a special case of Newton's method.

15.2 The pair of simultaneous equations quoted at the end of chapter 15 is an especially simple system which can be solved by eliminating y and solving a single equation for x. Use any appropriate method to find a solution (x, y) of the system. Are there any other solutions?

15.3 An equation $f(x) = 0$, where f is at least three times differentiable, has a real root at $x = \alpha$. An approximation x_0 is known for α. Expand $f(\alpha)$ in Taylor's series about x_0. By truncating at the first derivative and dropping the remainder term, devise a method for improving the approximation to α (the result should be familiar). Obtain a higher-order method by including the next term in the series. Use this method to solve the equation $x + \log_e x = 2$ correct to 4 decimal places on a calculator, and check by running `program Newton`.

15.4 Write a procedure to implement the bisection/secant algorithm described in section 15.3 (you should define a local constant as a multiple of the smallest positive real number - see remarks after the algorithm). Incorporate the procedure in a program and test on the equations of examples 15.2 and 15.3 (chapter 15) with various starting intervals. Compare the performance with that of the bisection method for a range of error tolerances.

16.1 Use `program TestPolysol`, or a modified version of it, to find individually all the real zeros of the cubic $2x^3 - 4x^2 - 3x + 4$ to full machine accuracy (remember to adjust the machine-dependent constants in procedure `Polysol`). Repeat for the polynomials $x^4 + x^3 - 7x^2 - x - 5$ and $8x^5 - 12x^4 + 6x^3 - 9x^2 - 2x + 3$.

16.2 Modify program `TestPolysol` with the aim of computing automatically all the real zeros of a polynomial as accurately as possible by the deflation method outlined at the end of section 16.2. Note that you will need to save a copy of the original polynomial coefficients for use in the refinement process, which has to be performed on every computed zero after the first. Do not forget that there may be fewer than n real zeros; you are not seeking complex zeros. Test on the polynomials of exercise 16.1.

17.1 Take program `PolyFit` out for a run. Some suggestions: fit a constant polynomial to 1, 2, ... data points; reproduce the results for straight line fitting in chapter 11; try to find a quadratic curve determined by 2 data points or by 3 points that happen to lie on a straight line. How does the program handle these cases - can you think of any improvements? Experiment with interpolation: fit a polynomial of degree n through any $n + 1$ distinct points for $n = 6, 7, 8, ...$. Can you account for the general behaviour as n increases?

17.2 Write a procedure which takes the results of procedure `LinSolve` - an array containing the multipliers and upper triangular form, and a vector containing the permuted row indices - and uses these to solve a system $Ax = b'$ with the same coefficient matrix but a different right hand side. Most of the work has been done already in `LinSolve`. Your procedure will need to rework the parts that depend specifically on the right hand side, and finally calculate the solution x.

Test on some 3×3 and 4×4 systems. Write a program that calls `LinSolve` once, then (provided the parameter `singular` has been returned as `false`) tries to solve systems with different right hand sides using the procedure you have written (you can easily make up suitable data by starting with known 'solutions'). Check that your procedure gives correct results in all cases.

17.3 The inverse of a nonsingular $n \times n$ matrix A can be computed as follows. The objective is to find an $n \times n$ matrix X satisfying $AX = I$, where I is the unit matrix. Take each column x_j of X and the corresponding column e_j of I, and solve the system $Ax_j = e_j$ (e_j is the column vector with jth component equal to 1, the other components equal to 0). Do this for $j = 1, ..., n$. Then set the resulting columns x_j side by side.

Write a program to compute a matrix inverse (if one exists) by this method. You will use procedure `LinSolve` for $j = 1$, but for $j > 1$ it will be much more efficient to use the procedure from exercise 17.2. Test on the matrices

$$\begin{bmatrix} 2 & 1 & 0 \\ 1 & 2 & 1 \\ 0 & 1 & 2 \end{bmatrix} \qquad \begin{bmatrix} 1 & -1 & 3 \\ 2 & 3 & -2 \\ 4 & 1 & 4 \end{bmatrix}$$

and check any results by hand. Then try some larger cases.

18.1 A table is required of the values of the integral $\int_0^\alpha x^2 e^{-x^2} dx$, correct to 4 decimal places, for $\alpha = 0.0$ (0.1) 2.0. Write a program to produce such a table by the modified Euler method.

18.2 Consider the initial value problem

$$d^2u/d\theta^2 + u = Ku^2$$

with $u = 1$ and $du/d\theta = 0$ at $\theta = 0$. As θ increases, it can be shown that u decreases. The problem is to find the value θ_0 at which $u = 0$. Solve this problem numerically for $K = 0.1$ as follows. Start at $\theta = 0$; using the modified Euler method for systems, take steps of 0.01 until u becomes negative; then move back one step and determine θ_0 more accurately by taking steps of 0.0001. Finally output the value of $2\theta_0 - \pi$, converted from radians to degrees and rounded to 2 decimal places.

The result is, in Einstein's theory of gravitation, the angle of deflection of a light ray passing close to the surface of a dense star (by comparison, for the sun $K \approx 6.4 \times 10^{-6}$).

18.3 The gun crew of example 18.3 are told to go back and do the job properly, this time firing at an elevation of θ degrees to the horizontal where $45 < \theta < 90$ (the sergeant-major is most explicit about the second inequality). If they can find the correct elevation $\bar{\theta}$ to score a direct hit on a target 1000 metres away, all will be forgiven.

The vector equation of motion is

$$\ddot{\mathbf{r}} = -\mathbf{g} - a\dot{\mathbf{r}} - b\dot{\mathbf{r}}|\dot{\mathbf{r}}|$$

with the same constants and initial velocity as before. Write this as a system of four first-order differential equations. Hence develop a program which will output a table showing the height and downrange distance of the shell throughout its flight. Experiment with the program to find the desired angle $\bar{\theta}$.

Appendix: Program Design

1. How Not To Do It

If you have to read and try to understand programs (even your own), you will soon appreciate the virtues of clear structure, sensible layout and informative commenting. The choice of layout convention does not really matter as long as it adequately reflects the logical structure and you stick to it. A little investment of time and thought pays dividends.

Consider the following piece of work handed in by a student (one of a large class for whose remarkable programming attainments the authors disclaim responsibility!)

```
PROGRAM DATAFIT(INPUT,OUTPUT,FIN,FOUT);
TYPE DATAVEC=ARRAY[0..100 OF REAL;
TYPE COEFFMAT ARRAY[0..100,0..100] OF REAL;
VAR M,N:INTEGER;
FIN,FOUT:TEXT;
X,F,P,Q,R:DATAVEC;
A;COEFFMAT;
PIVOT,MULT,SUM,RMS:REAL;
PROCEDURE SETUP(H,P:INTEGER;VAR D,E:DATAVEC;VAR G:COEFFMAT);
VAR I,J,J2:INTEGER;
   POWER:REAL;
BEGIN (*INITIALIS
ATOIN*)
G[0,P+1]:=0;
    FOR J:=  1 TO P Do
    BEGIN
        G[0,J]:=0;G[J,P]:=0;
        G{J,P+1]:= 0
    END;
(*ACCUMILATE SUMS IN MATRIX*)
FOR J:=1 TO P DO
BEGIN
```

```
   G[0,P+1]:=G[0,P+1]+E[I};
   POWER:=1;
   FOR j2:= 1 TO P DO
     BEGIN
POWER:=POWER*D[I];
A[0,J]:=G[0,J]+POWER;
G[J,P+1]:=G[J,P+1]+POWER*E[I]
END;
FOR J:= 1 TO P DO
BEGIN
   POWER:=POWER*D[I];
   G[J,P]:=G[J,P]+POWER;
END
END;
(*MATRIX A*)
G[0,0]:=H;
FOR J:=1 TO P DO
BEGIN
   FOR I: 1 TO J Do
   G[I,J-1]:=G[0,J];
   FOR I:=J+1 TO P DO
   G[I,P+J-1]:=G[J,P]
END
END;
PROCEDURE REDUCTION(Q:INTEGER;VAR B:COEFFMAT);
VAR K,I,J:INTEGER;
   PIVOT,MULT:REAL;
BEGIN
   FOR K:=0 TO Q-1 DO
   BEGIN
PIVOT:=B[K,K];
        FOR I:=K+1 TO Q DO
BEGIN
        IF PIVOT<>0 THEN MULT:=B[I,K]/PIVOT;
        FOR J:=K+1 TO Q+1 DO
        B[I,J]:=B[I,J]-MULT*B[K,J]
          END
   END
END;
PROCEDURE BACKSUBS(H:INTEGER;S:COEFFMAT;VAR Q:DATAVEC);
(*TO SOLVE EQNS FROM REDICTION PROCEDURE*0
VAR I,J:INTEGER;
   SUM:REAL;
   C:DATAVEC;
BEGIN
```

```
    FOR I:=H DOWNTO 0 DO
    BEGIN
SUM:=S[I,H+1];
    FOR J:=I+1 TO H DO
    SUM:=SUM-S[I,J]*Q[J];
    Q[I]:=SUM/S[I,I]
END
END;
BEGIN
    RESET(FIN);
    READLN(FIN,M);
    READLN(FIN);
    FORI:=1 TO M DO
        READLN(FIN,X[I],F[I]);
    WRITE('ENTER DEGREE POLYNOMIAL  TO BE FITTED.....':45)READLN(N);
.
IF N >=M THEN
WRITE('TOO MANY UNNOWNS':50)
ELSE
BEGIN
SETUP(M,N,X,F,A);
REDUCTION(N,A);
BACKSUBS(N,A,R)
END
END.
```

There followed a long list of compilation error messages, rounded off by a note inviting the marker to 'debug' the program. What would your answer have been? See if you can rewrite it (the program, not your well-chosen answer) so that it at least looks like a Pascal program.

2. Stepwise Refinement: A Football League Program

[*This draws on concepts from chapters* 7 & 8 *and section* 10.1]

We have been approached by the Hon. Secretary of the Leeds Local Soccer League to design a computer program which will maintain and update a football league table. This gentleman explained that, although there are only eight teams in the league this year, he expects that in view of the popularity of the sport there will be many more teams playing in future, and this will certainly make the job of manually updating the league table a lot more tedious and error-prone. 'All I want', he said, 'is a program that will produce something like this', and he showed us an example.

	P	W	D	L	F	A	P
Kirkstall Dynamo	2	1	1	0	8	3	4
Chapeltown Rovers	1	1	0	0	3	2	3
Headingley Forest	2	1	0	1	5	6	3
Roundhay Park Rangers	2	1	0	1	1	5	3
Moortown Athletic	1	0	1	0	3	3	1
Armley Gaol Wanderers	2	0	1	1	5	6	1
Lawnswood Cemetery	2	0	1	1	3	4	1
Yeadon High-fliers	2	0	1	1	4	5	1

Given such a table and a list of score lines, for example

Yeadon High-fliers 4   Chapeltown Rovers 2
Kirkstall Dynamo   0   Headingley Forest   3

the program should add the results to the statistics and produce an updated table. 'As you may know,' he informed us a trifle condescendingly, 'teams get 3 points for a win, 1 point for a draw and nothing if they lose. The teams are ranked according to their total points (P in the last column); teams with the same points are discriminated by goal difference (F − A column entries), and if they still cannot be separated they are listed in alphabetical order of team names. Oh, one more thing before I leave you to it', he added. 'Could you arrange it so that we don't have to specify the full team names when we type in the results: Kirk 0 Head 3 will do nicely. Thank you very much.'

We thought about the problem over a couple of pints to identify the various tasks involved, and came up with the following plan.

(1) GetTable: input an existing league table from a file, or create an initial table given a list of team names - presumably once at the start of each season.
(2) - - - - - - : save the table in a backup file before any changes are made.
(3) ProcessResults: read score lines from an input stream, validating them as they are read; if a line is syntactically correct, update the performance statistics, otherwise issue an error message and ignore the line.
(4) SortTable: sort the teams according to their ranking.
(5) - - - - - - - : display the updated and sorted table on screen.
(6) - - - - - - - : store the new table on file, overwriting the old table.

These tasks, we anticipated, would correspond to procedures in our program. It remained to fill in the details, that is, to refine each task as far as possible by splitting it into smaller, more manageable subtasks, until a level is reached where the subtasks can be coded and tested. Of crucial importance is the choice of data structure to represent a league table, and the decision as to how we should organize input and output (a poor choice at this stage can make program design much more difficult). This is what we will discuss first.

Data Structure

A league table consists of a fixed number of rows all of the same structure. It therefore seems appropriate to declare a variable Table of type

```
array[teamrange] of row
```

where

```
teamrange = 0..maxteams
```

(maxteams is the maximum number of teams allowed in the league; the reason for starting the range at 0 instead of 1 will become apparent later). The row structure can be represented by a record type (see section 10.1)

```
row = record
        team : teamname;
        played,
        won,drawn,lost,
        fore, against, points : integer
      end;
```

(note that we cannot use the obvious identifier for as a field name, since **for** is a reserved word). In the above definition, teamname is a string type suitable for holding the name of a team:

```
teamname = packed array[namerange] of char
```

where

```
namerange = 1..namelength
```

for some appropriate constant namelength.

The number of teams in the league is conveniently held in a variable numteams. This variable, like Table, is *global*, since once established it never changes and its value is required by most of the subprograms.

Input / Output Arrangements

An existing league table (or a list of teams preceded by the number 0 to indicate the start of a season) is read from a file associated with a program parameter newfile; a backup copy of the table is written to a file associated with a program parameter oldfile. The score lines are presented to the program via the standard input stream input (which, for convenience of data preparation, will normally be associated with a disk file, although input of results from the keyboard is possible). As always, the exact manner in which these associations are set up is system dependent.

We are now in a position to outline the basic structure of the program, i.e. the definitions and the main program body. Tasks (1) - (6) are represented by subprograms. One point we note immediately is that tasks (2), (5) and (6) are essentially the same and can be handled by a single procedure WriteTable, with a file parameter to designate the various output destinations.

```
program LeagueTable (input, output, oldfile, newfile);
const
   linelength  = 81;    (* maximum length of score line + 1 *)
   namelength  = 31;    (* maximum length of team name + 1  *)
   maxteams    = 20;    (* maximum number of teams in league *)
   space = ' ';
type
   linerange = 1..linelength;
   namerange = 1..namelength;
   teamrange = 0..maxteams;
   teamname  = packed array[namerange] of char;
   row       = record
                   team : teamname;
                   played,
                   won, drawn, lost,
                      fore, against, points : integer;
               end;
   buffer    = packed array[linerange] of char;

var
   Table    : array[teamrange] of row;      (** global   **)
   numteams : teamrange;                     (** variables **)
   oldfile,
    newfile : text;

<procedure GetLine>         (* see Data Input below *)
<procedure GetTable>
<procedure WriteTable>
<procedure SortTable>
<procedure ProcessResults>

begin     (* main program *)
writeln;
writeln('Football league program ...');
writeln;
GetTable(newfile);            (* input the league table *)
WriteTable(oldfile,1);        (* make backup copy *)
ProcessResults;               (* input match results and update table *)
SortTable;                    (* sort the table *)
WriteTable(output,2);         (* display it *)
WriteTable(newfile,3);        (* save it as newfile *)
writeln;
writeln('Old table saved in ''oldfile'', new table in ''newfile'' ')
end.
```

Data Input

For data input and analysis we need a buffer capable of holding an input line. For this purpose we define the data type

```
        buffer = packed array[linerange] of char
with
        linerange = 1..linelength
```

where linelength is a suitably chosen constant.

The user-supplied data to the program consists either of a list of team names or a list of score lines. These will be read line by line. Since a line may contain redundant or multiple spaces, or conceivably might be entirely blank, it is convenient to tidy up each input line as it is read, removing superfluous spaces and also identifying a blank line. We shall mark the end of the significant portion of a string by appending a character which will not normally occur in the input; for this we choose the null character chr(0). As a consequence, there is no need to record the actual length of a string and, moreover, an empty string or a blank line is easily identified by inspecting its first character.

Input of a line of text and simultaneous suppression of redundant spaces is carried out by the utility routine

```
procedure GetLine (var infile : text;  var line : buffer);
(* Reads a line of text from infile, suppressing any leading
   or multiple spaces; line[1]=chr(0) signifies a blank line *)
    var
        i : linerange;
        ch, lastch : char;
    begin
    i := 1; lastch := space;
    while not eoln(infile) and (i < linelength) do
        begin
        read(infile, ch);
        if (ch <> space) or (lastch<>space) then
            begin   (* accept character *)
            line[i] := ch;  lastch := ch;
            i := i+1
            end
        end;
    readln(infile);
    line[i] := chr(0);   (* end marker *)
    for i := i+1 to linelength do  (* pad with trailing spaces *)
        line[i] := space
    end (* GetLine *);
```

Writing a Table to an Output Stream

Before an existing table is updated, a backup copy is made. Subsequently
the updated table is displayed on screen, then saved in a file. These operations
are carried out by procedure WriteTable. The structure of this subprogram is
quite simple and its logic is easy to understand.

```
procedure WriteTable (var outfile : text;  callnumber : integer);
(* Outputs league table to outfile *)
    var
        i : teamrange;
    begin
    if callnumber <> 2 then (* rewriting 'output' can cause problems *)
        rewrite(outfile);    (* in some Pascal implementations *)
    writeln(outfile, numteams, ' teams in league');
    writeln(outfile, space:namelength, ' P  W  D  L  F  A  P');
    writeln(outfile);
    for i := 1 to numteams do
        with Table[i] do
            writeln(outfile, team, played:3, won:3, drawn:3, lost:3,
                             fore:3, against:3, points:3)
    end (* WriteTable *);
```

Inputting a Table

This task is performed by procedure GetTable. Input of an *existing* league table
is the reverse of writing a table to an output stream (note that after reading
numteams, two lines have to be skipped; these are the header and the blank line
written by procedure WriteTable). At the start of a season when there is no
existing league table and only a list of team names is available, GetTable sets up
an initial table with all statistics set to 0. The procedure knows when this is
required because the number of teams is specified as 0.

```
procedure GetTable (var infile : text);
(* Inputs league table from infile. If the file starts with 0,
   an initial blank table is set up *)

    var
        i    : teamrange;
        j    : namerange;
        line : buffer;

    begin
    reset(infile);
    readln(infile, numteams);   (* input number of teams *)
    if numteams = 0 then        (* set up initial table  *)
        while not eof(infile) do
```

```
          begin
          GetLine(infile, line);
          if line[1] <> chr(0) then    (* line is not blank *)
             with Table[numteams+1] do
                begin
                for j := 1 to namelength do    (* copy team name *)
                   team[j] := line[j];
                (* initialize values *)
                played := 0;
                won  := 0; drawn := 0;  lost := 0;
                fore := 0; against:= 0; points := 0;
                numteams := numteams+1
                end
          end
   else
      begin    (* read in existing table *)
      readln(infile); readln(infile); (* skip first two lines *)
      for i := 1 to numteams do
         with Table[i] do    (* get team and values for i-th row *)
            begin
            for j := 1 to namelength do
               read(infile, team[j]);
            readln(infile, played,won,drawn,lost,fore,against,points)
            end
      end
end (* GetTable *);
```

Sorting the League Table

Once a league table has been updated, the teams must be arranged according to
their new ranking. This is a relatively simple sorting problem which can be
tackled by modifying the insertion sort algorithm of example 7.2. Instead of
sorting a set of characters subject to the obvious order relation <, we are
required to sort a set of 'rows' on which an order relation higher is defined by
the well-known rules for ranking teams in a football league: team x is higher
than team y if x has more points than y, or if they have the same number of
points and x has a greater goal difference; if this still does not separate them,
alphabetical ordering is used. Here is the sort procedure with a boolean function
higher declared locally.

```
procedure SortTable;
(* Sorts the rows of the table in descending order of team rank *)
   var
      i, j : teamrange;
      save : row;
```

```
function higher (var x, y : row) : boolean;
(* returns true if and only if x.team ranks higher
   than y.team in the league *)
    var
        dx, dy : integer;
    begin
    higher := x.points > y.points;
    if x.points = y.points then (* same points   *)
        begin                    (* use goal difference *)
        dx := x.fore - x.against;
        dy := y.fore - y.against;
        higher := dx > dy;
        if dx = dy then              (* same difference *)
            higher := x.team < y.team (* use alphabetical ordering *)
        end
    end (* higher *);

begin  (* body of SortTable - compare with example 7.2 *)
Table[0].points := maxint;    (* stopper for insertion sort *)
for i := 2 to numteams do
    begin
    save := Table[i];  j := i;
    while higher(save, Table[j-1]) do
        begin
        Table[j] := Table[j-1];  j := j-1
        end;
    Table[j] := save
    end
end (* SortTable *);
```

Processing the Results

This task is performed by procedure ProcessResults, the heart of the entire
program and consequently the least trivial part. We can, however, split this
complicated task into simpler components. First we need to read a score line
from the input stream; then, provided the line is not blank, we validate it and
update the current table with the new result. This process is repeated until the
input stream is exhausted. A direct translation of this idea into Pascal is

```
procedure ProcessResults;
(* Accepts results from input, analyzing and processing each line.
   If a line is found to contain an error, a message is sent to output
   and the line is ignored *)

    var
        line : buffer;
```

```
<procedure Process>      (* see below *)

begin  (* body of ProcessResults *)
while not eof(input) do
   begin
   GetLine(input, line);
   if line[1]<>chr(0) then    (* line is not blank *)
      Process(line)
   end
end (* ProcessResults *);
```

Here we have again used the utility procedure GetLine discussed earlier which inputs a line and removes redundant spaces. The procedure Process first displays the current line and then analyzes (*parses*) it, attempting to extract the two team names and two scores. (The way this is done will be explained later.) If this is successful and if the team names are valid, i.e. can be located in the given table, then the table statistics are updated; if an error is discovered then an informative message is sent to output and the current line is ignored. This procedure, with the local subprograms which will be required, is as follows.

```
procedure Process (var line : buffer);
(* Analyzes a score line expected to be of the form
      Home Team  4   Away Team 2
   If a team name is missing or is not recognized, or if a score
   is missing, an error message is output and the line is ignored.
   Otherwise the league table is updated *)

var
   homeside, awayside   : teamname;
   homescore, awayscore : integer;
   homerow, awayrow     : integer;
   i      : linerange;
   error : boolean;

<procedure parse>

<function rownumber>

<procedure update>

begin  (* body of Process *)
writeln(line);   (* echo line to output *)
i := 1;    (* initialize line index i, a non-local variable
               to procedure parse *)
parse(homeside, homescore);   (* identify home side / score *)
parse(awayside, awayscore);   (* identify away side / score *)
(* if a team name is missing, parse returns an empty string;
   if a score is missing, parse returns -1 *)
```

```
(* validate *)
error := (homescore=-1) or (awayscore=-1);
if error then
    writeln('Missing score');
homerow := rownumber(homeside);  (* locate home side in table *)
awayrow := rownumber(awayside);  (* locate away side in table *)
(* if a team name is not found, rownumber returns 0 *)

if homerow = 0 then
    begin
    writeln('Home team not recognized'); error := true
    end;
if awayrow = 0 then
    begin
    writeln('Away team not recognized'); error := true
    end;

(* update or ignore *)
if error then
    begin
    writeln('*** result ignored ***'); writeln
    end
else
    begin
    update(homerow, homescore, awayscore);
    update(awayrow, awayscore, homescore)
    end
end (* Process *);
```

We have used a local function rownumber (with a string parameter corresponding to a possible team name) which attempts to locate the name in the table, returning the row index if the name is found and 0 otherwise. We have also used a local procedure update to perform the requisite updating of the table statistics. We shall describe these two subprograms first, and discuss the parsing procedure later.

The function rownumber has to scan the list of team names in the table until it either discovers that the given name is present, or it reaches the end without having found it. Such a process is called a *linear search* and is quite straightforward. What makes it slightly more complicated is the requirement that a team name should be recognized even if only an initial segment is given; for example, if Chapeltown Rovers is the full name, the strings Chapeltown, Chap or even C should be recognized. What we need is a boolean function equal to perform such a test; this may then be used in the linear search for the row number.

```
function equal (s, t : teamname) : boolean;
(* returns true if and only if string s is an initial segment
   of string t; s is known to consist of at least one character *)
   var
       j  : namerange;
       eq : boolean;
   begin
   j := 1;
   repeat  (* until two characters disagree
               or string s is exhausted *)
      eq := s[j]=t[j];
      j := j+1
   until not eq or (s[j]=chr(0));
   equal := eq
   end (* equal *);

function rownumber (team : teamname) : teamrange;
(* Determines the row index of team in the table. If team is not
   found, the value 0 is returned *)

   var
       i : teamrange;

   <function equal declared here>

   begin
   if team[1]=chr(0) then  (* empty string *)
      rownumber := 0
   else
      begin
      Table[0].team := team;  (* stopper for linear search *)
      i := numteams;
      while not equal(team, Table[i].team) do
         i := i-1;
      rownumber := i
      end
   end (* rownumber *);
```

The procedure for updating the statistics of the team currently in row i is straightforward. (Remember that 3 points are awarded for a win and 1 point for a draw.)

```
procedure update (i : teamrange; f, a : integer);
(* Updates row i of table with scores f for and a against *)
   begin
   with Table[i] do
```

```
   begin
   played := played+1;
   fore := fore+f;
   against := against+a;
   if f > a then    (* a win *)
      begin
      won := won+1;  points := points+3
      end
   else if f = a then   (* a draw *)
      begin
      drawn := drawn+1;  points := points+1
      end
   else
      lost := lost+1
   end
end (* update *);
```

Lastly, we describe the process of analyzing a score line. A valid result has the syntactic form *name number name number*, where *name* is a team name and *number* is a non-negative integer representing a score. We insist that *name* and *number* be separated by a space (this is to allow team names containing a sequence of digits). We do not require a space between *number* and *name*. Since three-digit scores are unrealistic (even in the Leeds Local League), we consider at most two-digit numbers as potential scores. Specifying a first score ≥ 100 will give rise to the error 'Away team not recognized' (and no wonder).

Of course, a score or a team name may be missing; it is the purpose of a parsing routine to discover this. Since *name* and *number* need to be identified twice in a given line, we introduce a procedure parse which analyzes the non-local string line starting at position i (a variable which is non-local to parse). The objective is to find a string, possibly containing spaces, terminated by a space and followed by a digit; then to find a number < 100 starting with this digit. The procedure returns a team name (or an empty string, i.e. a string starting with chr(0) if no team name was found), and a score of at most two digits (or −1 if no score was found). In order to recognize a digit it is convenient to declare a local boolean function

```
function digit (ch : char) : boolean;
(* checks if ch is a digit *)
   begin
   digit := ch in ['0'..'9']
   end;
```

Here, finally, is the parsing routine. It is worth studying this carefully; you may learn some useful programming techniques.

```
procedure parse (var side : teamname;  var score : integer);
(* Parses a score line (non-local string variable line) starting at
   position i (non-local), and attempts to extract team name / score.
   If no score is found then score is returned as -1;
   if no team name is found then side[1] := chr(0) *)

   var
      j : namerange;
      scorefound : boolean;

   <function digit declared here>

   begin
   j := 1;  score := -1;  side[1] := chr(0);  (* default values *)
   scorefound := digit(line[i]);
   while not scorefound and (line[i] <> chr(0)) do
      begin
      if (line[i]=space) and digit(line[i+1]) then (* a number next *)
         scorefound := true
      else if j < namelength then
         begin   (* copy character *)
         side[j] := line[i]; j := j+1;
         side[j] := chr(0)    (* advance terminator *)
         end;
      i := i+1
      end;

   if scorefound then
      begin
      score := ord(line[i])-ord('0');  (* convert *)
      if digit(line[i+1]) then    (* it's a two-digit score *)
         begin
         i := i+1;
         score := 10*score + ord(line[i])-ord('0')
         end;
      i := i+1;
      if line[i]=space then i := i+1  (* ready for away team *)
      end
   end (* parse *);
```

We have refined all the original tasks to levels where the constituent problems can be solved and coded as subprograms. The resulting routines have well-defined interfaces, that is, explicit parameter lists with full specifications of their operation. As a general principle, the subprograms can and should be tested separately and jointly at each appropriate level before being incorporated into the program structure on page 192. This is the essence of *top-down design*, one recommended method for developing reliable, structured programs.

Reserved Words in Pascal

The complete set of reserved words in standard Pascal is

and	array	begin	case	const	div
do	downto	else	end	file	for
function	goto	if	in	label	mod
nil	not	of	or	packed	procedure
program	record	repeat	set	then	to
type	until	var	while	with	

These may not be used as identifiers in a program. Any other sequence of letters and/or digits, starting with a letter, is a valid identifier. There is nothing to prevent a programmer from using identifiers such as real or integer (which are *not* reserved words), for example to redefine these data types, but for obvious reasons this is not recommended.

Further Reading

Programming

E.B. Koffman: *Problem Solving and Structured Programming in Pascal*, 3rd ed. (Addison-Wesley, 1989). This is one of a large number of introductory texts aimed at students of Computer Science. The problems and examples used to illustrate the principles of programming and program design are generally non-mathematical.

D.A. Watt: *The Professional Programmers 'Guide to Pascal* (Pitman, 1988). This slim volume summarizes and illustrates the syntax and semantics of Pascal in a systematic, concise manner: an invaluable reference both for students and for experienced programmers.

Numerical Analysis

R.L. Burden and J.D. Faires: *Numerical Analysis*, 4th ed. (PWS-Kent, 1989). This is a long book which covers almost the whole range of numerical methods, including those for the algebraic eigenvalue problem and for ordinary and partial differential equations, at an intermediate level of exposition. The emphasis is on algorithmic description with many examples from scientific applications.

C.F. Gerald and P.O. Wheatley: *Applied Numerical Analysis*, 4th ed. (Addison-Wesley, 1989). This covers much the same ground as the above reference at perhaps a slightly gentler pace. FORTRAN programs are collected at the end of each chapter, and Pascal versions are available in a separate supplement.

G.M. Phillips and P.J. Taylor: *Theory and Applications of Numerical Analysis* (Academic Press, 1973). This book focusses on a narrower area of numerical analysis but treats it in greater depth, with a somewhat more mathematical emphasis.

Index